Elizabeth David
on Vegetables

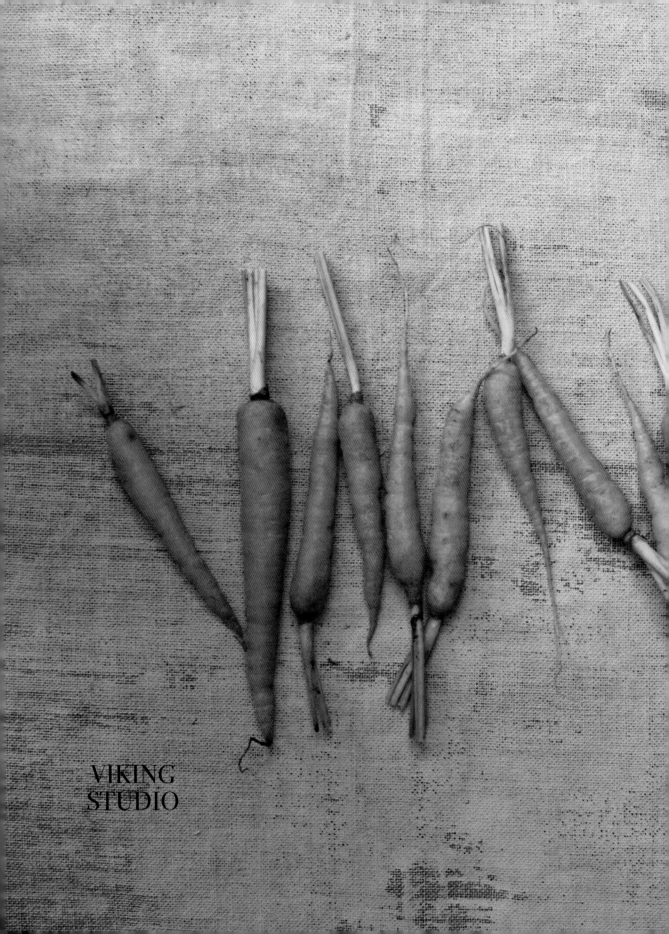

VIKING
STUDIO

Elizabeth David on Vegetables

Compiled by Jill Norman

Photography by Kristin Perers

"Of all the spectacular food markets in Italy, the one near the Rialto in Venice must be the most remarkable. The light of a Venetian dawn in early summer—you must be about at four o'clock in the morning to see the market coming to life—is so limpid and so still that it makes every separate vegetable and fruit and fish luminous with a life of its own, with unnaturally heightened colors and clear stenciled outlines. Here the cabbages are cobalt blue, the beets deep rose, the lettuces clear, pure green, sharp as glass."

These are the opening sentences of Elizabeth's description of the Venice market in *Italian Food*, published in 1954. She had an artist's eye and invites the reader to celebrate the sensual pleasures of food, whether of the market in Venice, the salad display of a barrow boy in Chinon, or a village girl in southern Spain preparing a tortilla for lunch. She taught us to see food in a new way, through her lyrical writing backed up by her years of experience in cooking, researching, and fact checking.

Between 1950 and 1960 she published five books on the food of the Mediterranean countries, Italy and France, of which *French Provincial Cookery* is still regarded as a masterwork on the subject. The books sold rapidly in cheap paperback editions and helped create a demand for Mediterranean fruit and vegetables. Chefs and domestic cooks acknowledged their influence. Many started up small restaurants with little more than an armful of Elizabeth David's books, pots and pans, enthusiasm, and good will. In addition she wrote regularly for *Vogue, Harper's Bazaar, House and Garden, The Dispatch, The Sunday Times, Wine and Food, The Spectator, Nova, Tatler*.

In the 1970s and '80s she wrote on English food: *Spices, Salt and Aromatics in the English Kitchen,* and *English Bread and Yeast Cookery,* and published a volume of essays and articles: *An Omelette and a Glass of Wine.* Later volumes of articles appeared posthumously. When *English Bread and Yeast Cookery* appeared in 1977, the publishers could not keep up with demand, nor could the mills producing stoneground flours.

Elizabeth's books contain many recipes in which vegetables are the main ingredient. In domestic cooking from northern France to the Mediterranean islands there are dishes of vegetables, rice, pasta, eggs, beans, lentils, and other legumes cooked with herbs and spices, local wine, and, depending on the region, butter, lard, or olive oil. I have made a selection of recipes from all of Elizabeth's books for *Elizabeth David on Vegetables.* Her dishes offer many ways to compose a vegetable or vegetarian menu, and they can of course be served with fish, meat, or poultry. There are delicate summer and satisfying winter soups, small dishes of fava beans in cream, fennel with Parmesan, or leeks in red wine and main dishes of pumpkin and tomato gratin, asparagus tart, or sweet-sour cabbage with prunes. The recipes are kept in the style in which they were written; if ingredients are listed they are put at the beginning of the recipe, other recipes remain in the narrative style.

Elizabeth's writing shows a self-effacing authority, and a passion and respect for authenticity and tradition; food is put into context, and she quotes widely from literature, history, travel writing. Her style is elegant, she writes with clarity and an imaginative boldness, with fire and bite and a caustic wit when the topic demands. She draws the reader in, making her or him want to cook, even if the instructions are sometimes sketchy. She expected readers to think for themselves, and not rely blindly on a recipe book.

Of one of her heroes, the Polish-French food writer Edouard de Pomiane, she wrote that his writing "is creative because it invites the reader to use his own critical and inventive faculties, form his own opinions, observe things for himself, instead of slavishly accepting what the books tell him." This could have been written of her own work.

She adhered to Escoffier's maxim "*faites simple*," noting that this did not mean that cooking could be done in a rush without any trouble. It also meant that she was against pretentiousness and fuss, outspoken about the bogus and the meretricious, about bad food. She had a stubborn integrity, she stood for honesty and authenticity, for using good-quality ingredients, and these were the principles of her cooking and her writing.

She brought a literary awareness to bear on food writing and created an environment in which the discussion of food became accepted in Britain, as it was in France, Italy, and elsewhere. Her writing placed her at the forefront of this "culinary enlightenment"; she led the way in turning food into an accepted topic for intellectual discussion, and food writing into an intellectual and respectable occupation. This was achieved entirely through her writing; Elizabeth was a private person, she avoided journalists seeking interviews, and her rare broadcasts on radio and TV were unsuccessful.

Widely read and formidably intelligent, writing was the medium she had chosen, and she would not be drawn away from it. Single-handedly she forged a British gastronomic tradition; her books paved the way for today's food writers and TV supercooks to find a receptive audience. Gastronomic studies, food history, food, and culture courses are increasingly on offer in our universities and colleges. Her enduring legacy is that the UK has some of the most adventurous food in the world.

2013 is the centenary of Elizabeth David's birth. I hope this collection of her vegetable dishes, published to celebrate the occasion, will lead readers familiar with her work to discover dishes they had overlooked, and will introduce younger readers to the work of this remarkable woman who did so much to improve British food.

Jill Norman FEBRUARY 2013

SOUPS

Minestrone Genovese
Genoese Minestrone

¾ cup of white haricot beans, 2 large eggplants, 1 pound of tomatoes, a cabbage, 2 or 3 zucchini or a piece of pumpkin, 3 ounces of fresh mushrooms or a few dried mushrooms, 3 tablespoons of olive oil, 3 ounces of pastine *or vermicelli, 2 tablespoons of pesto (p100), grated Parmesan.*

Boil the previously soaked haricot beans until they are three-quarters cooked. Strain them and put them into 3.5 quarts of fresh water. Add the peeled eggplants cut into squares, the peeled and chopped tomatoes, all the other vegetables cut into small pieces, and the olive oil. When the beans and the vegetables are all but cooked put in the pasta, and when it is tender stir in the pesto.

The vegetables for this minestrone can naturally be varied according to the season; carrots, cauliflower, green beans, celery, and potatoes can be added. The pesto makes Genoese minestrone one of the best of all.

Enough for eight.

Zuppa di vercolore
Green soup

An onion, olive oil, half a carrot, a small potato, 4 small tomatoes, half a cucumber or 2 or 3 zucchini, a little watercress, mint, ¼ pound of green beans, salt and pepper, a clove of garlic, a bunch of parsley.

Brown the sliced onion in olive oil, add the chopped carrot and potato, the skinned tomatoes also chopped, the diced cucumber or zucchini, the watercress, and mint. Season with salt and pepper and let them all simmer for a few minutes. Put in the green beans cut in small lengths, cover with 5 cups of water, and simmer until all the vegetables are cooked.

In the meantime pound the garlic and the parsley together with a little salt until they are a pulp. Stir this mixture into the soup a minute or two before serving.

Grated cheese to be served separately.

Enough for four or five.

Tuscan bean soup

Put scant 1½ cups of cannellini beans, or of pink borlotti beans, to soak in cold water. Leave them overnight.

Next day put the drained beans into a *fagiolara* (a flask-shaped Tuscan earthenware bean jar) or into a tall soup pan. Cover them with approximately 1.6 quarts of fresh cold water. Add 3 or 4 bay leaves, a teaspoon of dried savory or basil leaves (Tuscan cooks use sage. I find it too overpowering), 3 tablespoons of fruity olive oil.

Cook the beans, covered, over moderate heat for about 2 hours. Add a tablespoon of salt and continue cooking for another 20 to 30 minutes, until the beans are quite soft.

Now strain half the beans only, with about half the liquid, through a mouli-légumes food mill, or puree them in the blender, but not for long enough to get an unattractive electric-mixer-foam on the top; mix the puree with the rest of the beans, add a good fistful of parsley, coarsely chopped with a clove or two of garlic, and reheat the soup. Before serving, stir in a ladleful of fruity olive oil and the juice of a lemon.

In each soup plate or bowl have ready a slice of coarse country bread—or the nearest you can get to such a commodity—rubbed with garlic and sprinkled with olive oil.

This amount of beans should make enough soup for four.

La soupe
au pistou
Vegetable soup

A famous Niçois soup of which there are many versions, the essential ingredient being the basil with which the soup is flavored, and which, pounded to a paste with olive oil, cheese, and pine nuts makes the sauce called pesto so beloved of the Genoese. The Niçois have borrowed this sauce from their neighbors, adapted it to suit their own tastes, and called it in the local dialect, *pistou*. It is the addition of this sauce to the soup which gives it its name and its individuality. Without it, the soup would simply be a variation of minestrone.

Here is the recipe given in *Mets de Provence* by Eugéne Blancard (1926), a most interesting little collection of old provençal recipes.

In a little olive oil, let a sliced onion take color; add 2 skinned and chopped tomatoes. When they have melted, pour in 4 cups of water. Season. When the water boils throw in ½ pound of green beans cut into lengths, ¾ cup of white haricot beans (these should be fresh, but in England dried ones must do, previously soaked, and cooked apart, but left slightly underdone), a medium-size zucchini unpeeled and cut in dice, 2 or 3 potatoes, peeled and diced. When available, add also a few chopped celery leaves, and a chopped leek or two. After 10 minutes add 2 ounces of large vermicelli in short lengths.

In the meantime prepare the following mixture: in a mortar pound 3 cloves of garlic with the leaves of about 10 sprigs of fresh basil. When they are in a paste, start adding 2 or 3 tablespoons of olive oil, drop by drop. Add this mixture to the soup at the last minute, off the fire. Serve grated Parmesan or Gruyère with it.

Enough for four.

Zuppa pavese

Zuppa pavese appears regularly upon the menu of practically every restaurant in Italy. Rightly, for it is a capital invention, admirable when one is tired, and also for solitary meals, for it is not only quickly prepared but one dish provides the elements of a nourishing meal—broth, eggs, bread, cheese. You need vegetable, chicken, or meat consommé. Naturally the flavor of the consommé depends on the excellence of the result. You also need an egg per person, small slices of bread, and grated cheese.

While the consommé is heating up, fry your slices of bread (3 for each plate of soup) in butter. Poach the eggs in the hot consommé, lift them out into the heated plates, pour the consommé over them (through a fine strainer if there are any pieces of white of egg floating about). Spread a little grated cheese over each slice of fried bread, and arrange 3 around each egg. Serve more grated cheese separately.

Some Italian cooks break the eggs into the plates and simply pour the boiling consommé over them, but this method does not, to my mind, cook the eggs sufficiently.

Mayorquina

Majorca once belonged to the Catalan province which included the town of Perpignan, where the castle of the kings of Majorca is still to be seen. This traditional soup probably dates from those days. It has all the characteristics of the combined French and Spanish cooking of this region. It should be made in an earthenware marmite or casserole, which can be left to simmer either on top of a mat over the stove or in a slow oven.

You need ½ pound of ripe tomatoes, 1 red bell pepper, 5 or 6 cloves of garlic, 2 medium-size Spanish onions, 2 ounces of leeks, the heart of a small cabbage, 3 tablespoons of olive oil, a branch of thyme, a clove, a bay leaf finely chopped, salt, pepper.

Peel and slice the tomatoes. Remove the seeds and white pith from the pepper and cut it into strips. Clean and chop the other vegetables. Put the oil into the pan, which should not be so large that the oil disappears at the bottom, and when it is warmed put in the finely chopped garlic, then the onions, and the leeks. Let this simmer gently for 10 minutes, stirring with a wooden spoon so that the vegetables melt but do not brown. Now add the peeled and sliced tomatoes and the pepper cut into strips, simmer, and stir for another 15 minutes.

Now add slowly about 1.3–1.7 quarts of hot water and bring it to boiling point; at this moment add the chopped cabbage, the thyme, clove, and bay leaf, and salt and pepper, and cover the pan, letting it simmer for 1½ to 2 hours.

In the soup tureen place several large thin slices of brown or whole wheat bread. Before serving the soup, stir in a tablespoon of fresh olive oil and do not allow the soup to boil again. Pour it over the bread in the tureen, and be sure to have a pepper mill on the table so that each guest can season his soup to his own taste.

Enough for five to six people.

NOTE Today it would be more usual to put the bread into individual soup bowls.

Carrot soup

¾ pound of carrots, 1 shallot or half a small onion, 1 large potato, 2 tablespoons of butter, seasoning, 2½ cups of turkey, chicken, or vegetable stock, or water if no stock is available, parsley and chervil if possible.

Scrape the carrots, shred them on a coarse grater, put them together with the chopped shallot and the peeled and diced potato in a thick pan with the melted butter. Season with salt, pepper, a scrap of sugar. Cover the pan, and leave over very low flame for about 15 minutes, until the carrots have almost melted to a puree. Pour over the stock, and simmer another 15 minutes. Strain or blend, return the puree to the pan, see that the seasoning is correct, and add a little chopped parsley and chervil.

Enough for three.

NOTES

1. Sometimes boiled rice is served separately with this soup, which makes it pretty substantial. Fried bread crumbs or small dice of fried potatoes are alternatives.

2. It is of course important to have good-quality carrots, and both the taste and the color of the soup will depend on this, and will vary accordingly. Young carrots will give a clear, bright-orange color and a sweet flavor; later in the season the full-grown carrots will give a yellow soup and will probably need more sugar in the seasoning.

3. The consistency of the soup depends to a certain extent upon the quality of the potatoes, which makes it almost impossible to give an exact quantity for the stock.

Potage crème de petits pois

Cream of green pea soup

This is one of the nicest, freshest, and simplest of the summer soups. Those who claim not to be able to taste the difference between frozen and fresh peas will perhaps find it instructive to try this dish. Not that a very excellent soup cannot be made with frozen peas, but when fresh peas are at the height of their season, full grown but still young and sweet, the difference in intensity of flavor and of scent is marked indeed.

Quantities are 1¾ pounds of peas, the heart of the cabbage lettuce, ½ cup/1 stick (yes, ½ cup/1 stick) of butter, 4 cups of water, salt, and sugar.

Melt the butter in your soup saucepan; put in the lettuce heart washed and cut up into fine strips with a silver or stainless-steel knife; add the shelled peas, 2 teaspoons of salt, and a lump or two (about 1–1½ teaspoons) of sugar. Cover the pan; cook gently for 10 minutes until the peas are thoroughly soaked in the butter. Add the water; cook at moderate pace until the peas are quite tender. Strain them, or puree them in a liquidizer. Return to the pan and heat up. A little extra seasoning may be necessary but nothing else at all.

Enough for four ample helpings.

Pastenak and cress cream

This is a lovely soup, a welcome change from the routine watercress and potato soup. *Pastenak* is the medieval English word for parsnip, a corruption of the Latin *pastinaca*.

Ingredients for the soup—a French one in origin—are 1 pound of youthful parsnips (there should be six; don't buy large horny old roots. They are both wasteful and disagreeable in flavor), 2½ cups of thin, clear vegetable or chicken stock, salt, 1 level teaspoon of rice starch or fine ground rice, or potato starch, or arrowroot, 1 handful of mustard sprouts, ¼–⅓ cup of cream. To serve with the soup, a bowl of little croutons fried in clarified butter.

Scrub the parsnips. With a small sharp knife or a potato parer, prize out the hard little pieces of core from the crowns.

Put the parsnips in a saucepan with cold water just to cover. No salt at this stage. Boil them until they are soft—about 2 to 5 minutes. Remove them with a perforated spoon and let them cool on a dish. Keep the cooking water remaining in the saucepan. There will be about 1¼ cups, a valuable addition to the soup.

When the parsnips are cool enough to handle, the skins can be rubbed off, although personally I don't find this necessary. In the process of straining or pureeing in a blender or food processor, all skin will be smoothly incorporated.

Having, then, strained the parsnips through a stainless-steel wire strainer or whirled them in a blender, turn the resulting puree into a clean saucepan, stir in the reserved cooking water and the stock, adding a seasoning of salt—2 or 3 level teaspoons should be enough, but taste as you go.

Put the teaspoon of whichever starch you are using in a small bowl, ladle in a little of the warmed soup, stir to a smooth paste, return this to the saucepan, and stir well until the starch has done its work of binding the vegetable matter and the liquid content to a smooth but slightly thickened cream.

When the soup is hot, cut off the leafy tops of the cress with scissors, chop them small, stir them into the soup. Add the cream.

Have the croutons already fried in clarified butter and drained on paper towels. Serve them separately in a warm bowl.

There will be enough soup for five big cups.

Potage crème de tomates et de pommes de terre
Cream of tomato and potato soup

3 tablespoons of butter, the white part of 2 leeks, ½ pound of tomatoes, ¾ pound of potatoes, salt, sugar, a little cream, chervil, or parsley.

Melt the butter in a heavy saucepan; before it has bubbled put in the finely sliced leeks; let them just soften in the butter. Half the success of the soup depends on this first operation. If the butter burns or the leeks brown instead of just melting, the flavor will be spoilt.

Add the roughly chopped tomatoes; again let them cook until they start to give out their juice. Add the peeled and diced potato, a seasoning of salt, and 2 lumps (about 1–1½ teaspoons) of sugar. Cover with 3 cups of water. After the soup comes to a boil, let it simmer steadily but not too fast for 25 minutes. Blend and strain or put it through the food mill, twice if necessary. Return the puree to the rinsed-out saucepan. When it is hot, add about ½ cup of cream. In warm weather it is advisable first to bring this to a boil, as if it is not quite fresh it is liable to curdle when it makes contact with the acid of the tomatoes. Immediately before serving stir in a little chervil or very finely chopped parsley.

For all its simplicity and cheapness this is a lovely soup, in which you taste butter, cream, and each vegetable, and personally I think it would be a mistake to add anything to it in the way of individual fantasies. It should not, however, be thicker than thin cream, and if it has come out too solid the addition of a little milk or water will do no harm.

The chef's soup known as *potage Solférino* is based on this puree of tomatoes, leeks, and potatoes but is complicated—needlessly to my mind—with a final addition of little pieces, of green beans and tiny marbles of potatoes scooped from large ones with a special implement.

Enough for four good helpings.

Potage cressonnière à la crème

Cream of watercress and potato soup

A richer version of the potato and watercress soups found in household cooking all over France. Peel 1 pound of potatoes and cut them into even sizes but not too small, or they will become watery. Even so elementary a dish as potato soup is all the better for attention to the small details. Boil them in 1.3 quarts of salt water, adding the stalks of a bunch of watercress. Keep the leaves for later. As soon as the potatoes are quite soft, after about 25 minutes, strain the whole contents of the pan through the food mill, using the medium mesh, or blend. Mix a tablespoon of rice flour (*crème de riz*) or potato flour (*fécule*) to a paste with a little of the soup; add this to the rest, heat gently, and simmer 25 minutes; strain again, this time through the fine mesh. The result should be quite a smooth cream, more cohered than the usual potato soup in which the potatoes always tend to separate from the liquid. Before serving add a pinch of nutmeg, about 2 tablespoons of finely chopped watercress leaves, and a good measure of cream, say about ⅔ cup. The result is a soup of the delicate coloring and creamy texture of so many of the dishes which charmed me when I first experienced French cooking with a Norman family.

Plenty for four.

Pumpkin and celery soup

Cheap, easy, mild, but quite an original and distinguished soup. Don't make it more than a day in advance—pumpkin tends to sour rather quickly. Serve it before red meat and game roasts, hot or cold; ham, pork, broiled or fried chicken, or baked or broiled fish. Avoid melon, marrows, and pale creamy sauces in the rest of the dishes.

3 cups of milk, 2 pounds of pumpkin, a stalk of celery or the leaves of a whole small head, salt, 2½ cups of mild stock or water, butter, lemon juice, parsley.

Bring the milk to a boil and let it cool a little. Peel the pumpkin and discard the seeds and cottony center. Cut roughly into small pieces and put in a large saucepan with the celery cut into small pieces and a scant tablespoon of salt. Cover with the stock or water and the strained milk. Simmer for about 30 minutes until the pumpkin is tender. Strain or blend. Return to the pan, and when reheating, add, if the soup is too thick, a little more stock or milk, stir in a good lump of butter, a squeeze of lemon juice, and some chopped parsley.

There will be enough soup for six helpings.

Garlic Presses are Utterly Useless

According to the British restaurant guides, dining at John Tovey's Miller Howe Hotel on Lake Windermere is an experience akin to sitting through the whole *Ring Cycle* in one session. Perhaps, but in Tovey's latest book, *Feast of Vegetables*, there is little sign of excess or eccentricity. His recipes are basically conventional, the novelty, and it is a useful one, lying in the seasonings. Carrots may be spiced with coriander or caraway seed, or green ginger. Orange juice and rind go into grated beet. Marsala and toasted almond slivers give zucchini a new look and a new taste. Chicory or Belgian endives are braised in orange juice, the grated peel added. A celery root soup is again flavored with orange juice and the grated rind. A celery root, zucchini, and potato mixture is cooked in a skillet into a flat cake—a useful recipe for nonmeat-eaters. Another in the same category is for individual molds of cooked carrots and turnips, whizzed into a puree with hazelnuts, egg yolks, cream, and seasonings of onion salt (something I can myself at all times do without), and ground ginger. Whisked egg whites are folded in, the mixture is transferred to buttered ramekins lined with lettuce leaves, baked in a hot-water bath in a hottish oven, and turned out for serving. All oven temperatures are given in Fahrenheit, centigrade, and gas marks, and timing is always carefully worked out, in many cases with three alternatives, according to whether you want your vegetables crisp—Tovey steers clear of the idiotic term "crispy"—firm or soft.

It is when we get to the subject of garlic that I really warm to Mr Tovey. What he has to say about its preparation is alone worth the price of his book. The passage should be reproduced in large type, framed, and sold in gift stores for the enlightenment of gadget-minded cooks the length and breadth of the land. In the manner of those pious thoughts which once adorned the walls of cottage parlors, proclaiming that "God is Love," or "Drink is the Pick-me-up which lets you Down," Mr Tovey's text is concise and to the point. Readers, heed him *please*: "I give full marks to the purveyors of garlic presses for being utterly useless objects."

I'd go further than that. I regard garlic presses as both ridiculous and pathetic, their effect being precisely the reverse of what people who buy them believe will be the case. Squeezing the juice out of garlic doesn't reduce its potency; it concentrates and intensifies the smell. I have often wondered how it is that people who have once used one of these diabolical instruments don't notice this and forthwith throw the thing into the trash can. Perhaps they do but won't admit it.

Now here is John Tovey again. The consistency you're looking for when adding garlic to a dish is "mushy and paste-like." Agreed. It is quickly achieved by crushing a peeled clove lightly with the back edge of a really heavy knife blade. Press a scrap of salt into the squashed garlic. That's all. Quicker, surely than getting the garlic press out of the drawer, let alone using it and cleaning it. As a one-time kitchen-store owner who in the past has frequently, and usually vainly, attempted to dissuade a customer from buying a garlic press, I am of course aware that advice not to buy a gadget which someone has resolved to waste their money on is usually resented as bossy, ignorant, and interfering. At least now I am not alone.

Now a word of dissent. If there's one thing about expensive restaurant cooking which to my mind spoils vegetable soups, it's the often unnecessary and undesirable use of chicken or meat-based stock as a foundation. John Tovey uses just one basic chicken or turkey and vegetable stock for every one of his soups, from asparagus, zucchini, fennel, and Jerusalem artichoke to parsnip, corn, tomato, turnip. I suppose that passes in a hotel restaurant where you're feeding different people every day, but in household cooking such a practice soon results in deathly monotony.

That's one, just one, of the reasons that stock cubes are so awful. They give the same underlying false flavor to every soup. It can't be sufficiently emphasized that many vegetable soups are best without any stock at all. It's not a question of lazy cooking. Years and years ago I learned from Boulestin not to diminish and distort the indefinably strange and alluring flavor of Jerusalem artichoke puree with stock. A year or two ago, when Raymond Blanc was still at the Quat' Saisons in Oxford, I had there a creamy pumpkin soup which I'd be happy to eat every other day. He told me he used a very light vegetable stock as a base for his delectable creation. The information seems worth passing on.

Minestra di lenticchie e pasta
Lentil soup with pasta

A warming winter soup.

A medium-size onion, olive oil, 3 or 4 large tomatoes, several cloves of garlic, a stalk of celery, scant 1 cup of brown lentils, salt, pepper, a bunch of parsley or mint, 2 quarts of water, 2 ounces of pastine (pasta made in the shape of long grains of rice) or broken-up spaghetti.

Fry the thinly sliced onion in olive oil, then add the peeled and quartered tomatoes, the chopped garlic, and the celery cut into short lengths. After 5 minutes put in the lentils and stir them so that they absorb the oil. Season them, and add the parsley or mint. Pour over 2 quarts of hot water, and let the soup cook fairly fast for about an hour, when the lentils should be done. Throw in the pasta and cook for 10 minutes more.

Enough for six people.

Potage de lentilles à l'oseille
Lentil and sorrel soup

Cook scant ⅔ cup of green or brown lentils in 1.3 quarts of water until the lentils are quite tender, adding salt only toward the end. Add about ¼ pound of sorrel, washed, chopped, and cooked in butter; blend or strain the whole mixture. Heat up, and if too thick add more water or, better, a little stock; taste for seasoning—a little sugar may be necessary. Stir in a good lump of butter before serving.

Enough for four.

NOTE Watercress may quite successfully be used instead of the sorrel.

SMALL DISHES

Tahini salad	Pound a clove of garlic in a mortar; stir in a cup of *tahini* paste, salt, pepper, half a cup of olive oil, half a cup of water, lemon juice, and coarsely chopped parsley. The *tahini* should be of the consistency of cream. In Egypt and Syria a bowl of *tahini* is served either with pre-lunch drinks or as an hors-d'oeuvre, with pickled cucumbers, pickled turnips, and the flat round bread (*Esh Baladi*) of the country. The *tahini* is eaten by dipping the bread into the bowl.
	NOTE This salad can be made more quickly in a food processor.
Eggplant puree	Broil or bake 4 eggplants until their skins crack and will peel easily. Strain the peeled eggplants, mix them with 2 or 3 tablespoons of yogurt, the same of olive oil, salt, pepper, lemon juice. Garnish this with a few very thin slices of raw onion and chopped mint leaves. This is a Middle Eastern dish which is intended to be served as a dip for bread, or with meat, in the same manner as a chutney.
L'aïllade toulousaine	Pound scant 1 cup of skinned walnuts in a mortar with 2 or 3 cloves of garlic; season them with a little salt. Add drop by drop at first, and then more quickly, about ½ cup of olive oil, stirring until you have a thick sauce.
	To be served with fresh bread and raw celery to dip in the *aïllade*, or as a sauce with any cold meat. Goes particularly well with tongue.
	NOTE The *aïllade* can be made in a food processor if you prefer.

Waiting for Lunch

In *French Country Cooking* there is a four-line description of *el pa y all*, the French Catalan peasant's one-time morning meal of a hunk of fresh bread rubbed with garlic and moistened with fruity olive oil. When the book first appeared in 1951, one reviewer remarked rather tartly that she hoped we British would never be reduced to breakfasting off so primitive a dish. I was shaken, not to say shocked—I still am—by the smug expression of British superiority and by the revelation, unconscious, of the reviewer's innocence. Believing, no doubt, that a breakfast of bacon and eggs, sausages, toast, butter, marmalade, and sweetened tea has always been every Englishman's birthright, she ignored countless generations of farm laborers, millworkers, miners, schoolboys, whose sole sustenance before setting off for a long day's work was nothing more substantial than a crust of coarse bread or an oatcake broken up in milk, buttermilk, or when times were good, in thin broth, when bad in water. The bread and olive oil of the southern European peasant was simply the equivalent of those sparse breakfasts of our own ancestors.

Recording some of the older recipes and meals of the country people of rural France was an exercise I had found most stimulating and instructive. There were ideas which often proved helpful in those days of shortages and strict rationing. It was not my intention to imply that we should copy those ideas to the letter—to do so at the time would hardly have been possible—but rather that we should learn from them, adapt them to our own climate and conditions, and perhaps benefit from increased knowledge of other people's diets and food tastes.

During the 25 years odd since the book was first published, we have indeed taken to imported dishes and cooking in a way which in 1951 would have seemed entirely in the realm of fantasy. One obvious example is the Neapolitan pizza—or rather, a tenth-rate imitation of it—now big business and familiar in every commercial deep freeze and takeout store in the land. And the original pizza, after all, was nothing more complicated than a by-product of the days of household bread-baking, when a few pieces of dough were kept back from the main batch, spread with oil and some kind of savory mixture—onions usually—baked in the brick oven after the bread was taken out, and devoured by hungry children and farm workers. That the pizza was not so far removed from the French and Catalan *pa y all* (the cooking of Catalonia was at one time closely related to that of southern Italy and Sicily) was demonstrated by a recent incident in a very ordinary restaurant in the town of Vendrell, a few miles across the Spanish frontier. Stopping one fall morning in 1976 for an early lunch, we saw the people at a neighboring table devouring some very appetizing-looking, aromatically smelling thick slices of warm bread spread with tomato and oil. We asked for the same. It was, of course, a version of *el pa y all*. Those slices of garlic-scented, oil-saturated bread, just lightly spread with a little cooked tomato, turned out to be the best item on the menu. You might think that doesn't say much for the restaurant's cooking, and that could be a fair criticism. What was interesting was that, not only were the local people eating it, but it was also the most expensive dish on the menu. The necessity of the day-before-yesterday's peasant has become the prized specialty of today's middle-class restaurant.

I don't think, however, that *el pa y all* will ever achieve popularity in England, at any rate not popularity on the scale reached by the pizza. We must be thankful for that, although for reasons rather different from those clearly in the mind of my reviewer of so long ago. As a nation we have a curious distrust of the primitive and simple in food, and so carefree a way with the specialties of other countries that while retaining the names, we have no inhibitions about complicating, altering, travestying, and degrading the dish itself. It is not difficult to visualize the fate of the *pa y all* if translated into English restaurant terms. It would become chopped garlic on toast made from factory bread, spread with salad cream, and crowned with a pepper-stuffed olive (that is the Catalan part, we should be told). In time, a very short time probably, this creation would find its way into the nation's deep-freeze. There would be a curry version and a cheese variation and a super-gigantic one with bacon, lettuce, onion rings, and radishes. Before long it would be more like an imitation Scandinavian open-face sandwich than the Mediterranean agricultural laborer's early morning breakfast.

El pa y all	The breakfast dish of the Catalan peasants in the Roussillon district of France. A piece of bread fresh from the baker (or sometimes fried in oil or pork fat), is rubbed all over with a piece of garlic, as little or as much as you like; then sprinked with salt, then a few drops of fresh olive oil, and the *pa y all* is ready.
Peperoni alla piemontese *Piedmontese peppers*	Cut some red, yellow or green bell peppers, or some of each if they are obtainable, in half lengthwise. Take out all the seeds and wash the peppers. If they are large, cut each half in half again. Into each piece put 2 or 3 slices of garlic, 2 small sections of raw tomato, about half a fillet of anchovy cut into pieces, a small nut of butter, a dessertspoon of oil, a very little salt. Arrange these peppers on a flat baking dish and cook them in a moderate oven for about 30 minutes. They are not to be completely cooked; the peppers should in fact be *al dente*, the stuffing inside deliciously oily and garlicky. Serve them cold, each garnished with a little parsley.

Eggplants à la Tunisienne

Tunisian eggplants

2 eggplants weighing approximately 6 ounces each, salt,
4 tablespoons of olive oil, 1 medium-size onion, 1 clove of garlic,
¾ pound of tomatoes, ½ teaspoon of ground allspice, a teaspoon of
dried basil or mint, cayenne, pepper, a tablespoon of currants,
a tablespoon of chopped parsley.

Cut the unpeeled eggplants lengthwise into 4 pieces and then into cubes. Put them in a colander, sprinkle them with salt, put a plate and a weight on top, and let them drain for an hour or so.

Heat the oil in a heavy skillet, put in the sliced onion, and cook gently until pale yellow and transparent. Now put in the eggplants, shaken dry in a cloth. Let them brown a little on each side; put in the garlic, crushed and broken into 3 or 4 pieces. Cover the pan and cook gently for about 15 minutes. Now add the skinned and chopped tomatoes, the allspice, the dried basil, a scrap of cayenne, and a little freshly ground black pepper, and cook until the moisture from the tomatoes has almost evaporated. Stir in the currants, which should have been previously soaked in a cup of water for a few minutes, and the parsley. The whole cooking time, after the eggplants are put in the pan, is from 25 to 30 minutes, and all the vegetables should be well amalgamated without being in a puree; and there should be a small amount of sauce.

Turn into a shallow bowl or serving dish. This dish is equally good hot or cold.

Enough for three to four people.

Eggplants with garlic, olive oil, and tomatoes

2 or 3 average-size eggplants, preferably long rather than round—say about 3 pounds weight in all—leaves discarded but stalks left intact, salt, 1 pound of tomatoes, about 4 cloves of garlic, 2 scant teaspoons of mixed ground spice—cinnamon, cloves, nutmeg, allspice, fresh basil or mint, sugar, approximately 8–10 tablespoons of olive oil.

Slash the unpeeled eggplants lengthwise and all around, without separating them at the stalk end, sprinkle them with salt. Skin the tomatoes and chop them with the peeled and crushed garlic cloves.

Put the eggplants into a casserole or baking dish with a lid, in which they will just fit lengthwise. Put tablespoons of the chopped tomatoes between each eggplant division until all is used up. Sprinkle in the mixed spice, a few cut or torn leaves of basil or mint, a little more salt, a teaspoon or two of sugar. Pour in olive oil to come at least level with the tops of the eggplants. Cover the pot. Cook in a low oven, 340°C, for approximately an hour. The eggplants should be soft but not mushy, and the sauce still runny. Taste the sauce for seasoning and if necessary add more salt and/or spice. Serve cold, with a little fresh basil or mint sprinkled over.

Enough for four as a first course.

NOTE This is basically the Turkish *Imam Bayeldi* but without the onions characteristic of that celebrated dish.

Fava beans and artichokes	Cook separately 2 pounds of fava beans and 8 artichoke bottoms. Strain the vegetables, keeping a little water in which the beans have cooked.

Heat 2 tablespoons of olive oil in a pan, stir in a very little cornstarch, half a cup of the water in which the beans were cooked, the juice of a lemon, some chopped parsley, and add the artichokes and fava beans.

Enough for four.

Fèves à la crème
Fava beans
with cream

3 tablespoons of butter, 2 pounds of very young fava beans, a teaspoon of flour, sugar, pepper, salt, ¼ cup of cream.

Melt the butter, put in the fava beans, and stir until they have absorbed most of the butter. Sprinkle with the flour, stir again, and just barely cover the beans with hot water. Add pepper and sugar, but salt only when the beans are practically cooked. Simmer steadily for 15 minutes, then stir in the cream previously boiled in another pan.

Enough for four.

Green beans with egg and lemon sauce

1 pound of green beans, 2 eggs, a lemon, olive oil, a tablespoon of grated Parmesan cheese.

Cook the beans in boiling salted water; drain them, setting aside about a cup of the water in which they have been cooked. Keep them hot. Have ready the eggs whisked to a froth with the lemon juice, a tablespoon of olive oil, and the cheese. Add a little of the water from the vegetables and heat this sauce over low flame, whisking all the time until it has thickened a little. It will only take a minute or two. Pour over the beans and serve at once. Also good cold.

Enough for four.

Cèpes à la bordelaise
Porcini with garlic and parsley

Wash the porcini and take the stalks off. If the porcini are large ones cut them in 2 or 3 pieces. Put a glass of good olive oil in a sauté pan and when it is hot put in the porcini. Let them brown a little, then turn the fire down very low. In the meantime, chop the stalks finely with a handful of parsley and as much garlic as you like. Sauté this mixture in a separate pan, also
in oil, then add it to the porcini. They need about 25 to 30 minutes' cooking.

This method of cooking can be applied to all kinds of mushrooms.

Ragoût of mushrooms and eggs

Put about ½ pound of sliced mushrooms into a pan with a little water, bring them to a boil, and add ⅔ cup of white wine. Season with salt, and a discreet amount of ground black pepper, nutmeg, and herbs.

Let the ragoût boil again for 2 or 3 minutes; and meanwhile have hot in a dish 5 or 6 hard-boiled eggs, roughly chopped, and a few plainly broiled whole mushrooms.

Pour the ragoût over the eggs, garnish with the broiled mushrooms, and serve at once.

An excellent dish, either to start the meal or as the vegetable course after cold meat or game, or as a main luncheon dish.

Enough for two to three.

Uova mollette con funghi e formaggio
Eggs with mushrooms and cheese

Prepare 2 eggs for each person, putting them into boiling water and cooking them for 5 minutes only so that the yolks remain soft, while the whites are firm. Shell the eggs as soon as they are cool enough to handle. The operation is easier if you crack the shells gently all over with the back of a knife before starting to peel them. For 4 eggs wash and slice ¼ pound of mushrooms and cook them in butter in a fireproof egg dish. When they are nearly ready put the shelled eggs into the pan, add more butter if necessary, and turn the eggs gently over two or three times so that they get hot, but they should cook as little as possible. Cover the eggs and the mushrooms with grated Parmesan, and serve as soon as this has melted, which should take about half a minute.

Enough for two.

Uova al piatto con pomidoro
Eggs and tomatoes

Remove the skins from 1 pound of tomatoes. Into a shallow, two-handled egg dish pour a small cup of olive oil, and in this fry a sliced onion. When it is golden add the chopped tomatoes and stew them for about 15 minutes, seasoning with salt, pepper, garlic if you like, nutmeg, fresh basil, or parsley. When the tomatoes are reduced more or less to a pulp break in the eggs (4) and cover the pan. The eggs will take about 6 or 7 minutes to cook and should be left until you see the whites are set and the yolks are soft. From the moment the eggs are put in, the dish can alternatively be put, covered, in a medium hot (350°F) oven.

Enough for two.

Zucchini
aux tomates
Zucchini
with tomatoes

1 pound of small zucchini, olive oil, ½ pound of tomatoes, garlic, salt, pepper.

If the zucchini are very small, simply wash them and leave them unpeeled. If they are the larger, coarser variety, pare off the rough ridge parts of the skin, so that the zucchini present a striped appearance. It is a pity to peel them entirely, for there is flavor in the skins. Slice them across on the bias, about ¼ inch thick. Heat 2 tablespoons of olive oil in a heavy skillet or sauté pan and put in the zucchini. Add a crushed clove of garlic. Let them cook, not too fast, until they have softened, turning them over with a spatula and shaking the pan from time to time so that they do not stick. Now add the skinned and roughly chopped tomatoes and, when these have softened and turned almost to a sauce, season with salt and a little freshly milled pepper, and turn onto a serving dish.

Nice as a separate vegetable, as an accompaniment to veal or lamb, or cold as an hors-d'oeuvre.

Enough for two or three.

Zucchini
à la niçoise
Zucchini with
tomatoes and
black olives

Cook the zucchini exactly as in the above recipe, and when they are ready, add about half a dozen pitted and halved black olives and a sprinkling of parsley.

Zucchini in
agrodolce
Zucchini in
sour-sweet sauce

Cut the unpeeled zucchini into circles. Cook them gently in a little olive oil with a cover on the pan; when they are nearly cooked, season with ground black pepper, a little powdered cinnamon, salt if necessary, and (for 1 pound of zucchini) 2 tablespoons of mild wine vinegar, and a tablespoon of sugar. Cook them a few minutes more. There should be a small amount of sauce, rather syrupy.

Enough for two or three.

Artichauts à la barigoule

Leaf artichokes braised in oil

This method of cooking artichokes seems to be one of the oldest of Provençal dishes. There are many versions, and in the course of time it has been elaborated to include all sorts of extra ingredients, but Provençal cooks mostly agree that it is best in its primitive form. The result is not unlike the famous *carciofi alla giudia* of Roman taverns, although the method is different.

Rather small young artichokes (the long, violet-leaved variety is the most common in Provence) in which the choke has not yet formed should be used. Rub the artichokes all over with lemon; cut off the stalks, leaving about ½ inch. Then cut off about ¾ inch from the top end of the artichokes, and remove about two layers of the outer leaves. Put them in a saucepan or sauté pan or deep skillet. Pour in olive oil to come halfway up, then cover with water. Turn the heat as high as possible so that the oil and the water come rapidly to a fast boil (it is the same method as used for the bouillabaisse) and amalgamate. Let it continue boiling, spluttering, and crackling (uncovered) for the whole cooking time, which is from 15 to 20 minutes, according to the size of the artichokes. Toward the end, you can see that the artichokes have turned golden brown and crisp and the outer leaves have spread out. Finally, the liquid will stop spluttering because all the water has evaporated, leaving only the oil. Take out the artichokes, and arrange them, stalks in the air, on a hot dish, so they look like beautiful bronzed little flowers, with the crisped petals spread out. Sprinkle over a little of their cooking liquid and some salt.

Allow two artichokes per person if they are small.

| Haricots verts à l'italienne | Boil the beans in salted water, keeping them rather undercooked. Cover the bottom of a small pan with olive oil, and when it is warm put in the strained beans; add for 1 pound of beans, 2 or 3 chopped tomatoes, and a little chopped garlic. Cook gently, shaking the pan from time to time for about 10 minutes, until the tomatoes have melted. |

Green beans with tomatoes and garlic

Enough for four.

| Cabbages stewed in butter with cream | The sketchy outlines of this excellent little dish are given in *The Dudley Book*, a collection of recipes put together by Georgiana, Countess of Dudley, and published in 1909. |

Ingredients are 3–4 tablespoons of butter, 1 small, very fresh crinkly green cabbage, 2 tablespoons of cream, seasonings of salt, vinegar, pepper, and nutmeg.

Trim off the outside leaves of the cabbage, slice the rest, fairly thinly, discarding the hard center stalk. Put the sliced leaves in a colander and rinse in cold water.

Heat the butter in a saucepan, put in the cabbage, stir it around, add a little salt, let it stew gently for about 5 minutes, stirring most of that time.

Now add the cream and cook for another 2 to 3 minutes. Sprinkle in a few drops of wine vinegar, then light seasonings of nutmeg and freshly milled pepper. Serve very hot while the cabbage is still crisp.

With a baked ham slice or a few sausages this makes a good, quickly cooked lunch dish.

Enough for four.

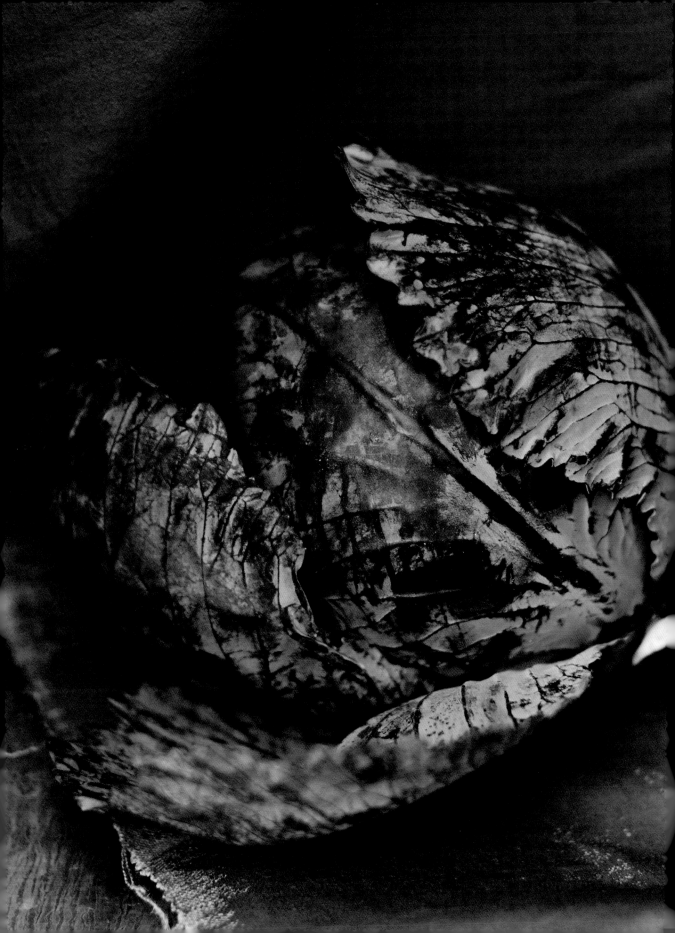

Poireaux au vin rouge
Leeks with red wine

Unexpectedly, perhaps, when wine is to be used in the cooking of leeks, the French always use red rather than white wine.

Choose small leeks, all of a size. Having cut them down almost to the white part and cleaned them thoroughly, put them side by side in a skillet in which you have heated 3 or 4 tablespoons of olive oil. As soon as they have taken color on one side, turn them over. Season with very little salt. Pour over them, for 1 pound of leeks, a wine glass of red wine (look out for the spluttering), let it bubble, add 2 tablespoons of good stock, or water if no stock is available, cover the pan, and cook at a moderate pace for 7 to 10 minutes, turning the leeks over once during the process. They are done when a skewer pierces the root end quite easily. Put the leeks in a shallow oval dish, cook the sauce another few seconds until reduced, and pour over the leeks.

Serve hot as a separate vegetable course, or cold as an hors-d'oeuvre. This is an example of a dish for which one would not buy wine especially, but which is delicious if you happen to have a glass to spare. It is a dish of particularly beautiful appearance, with the green of the leeks and the dark purple of the wine sauce.

Enough for three or four.

Endives au beurre

Chicory braised in butter

Allow 1½ to 2 endives per person. Peel off any brown outside leaves; wipe the endives with a cloth. With a stainless-steel knife cut each into ½-inch lengths. Melt a good lump of butter in a skillet. Put in the vegetables; let them cook a few seconds, turning them about with a wooden spoon before adding salt, turning down the heat, and covering the pan. By this method they will be sufficiently cooked in about 10 minutes (as opposed to over an hour when they are cooked whole), but uncover them and shake the pan from time to time to make sure the endives are not sticking. Before serving add a squeeze of lemon juice.

A variation is to add a few little cubes of bacon or ham. Leeks are excellent prepared and cooked in the same way.

Florentine fennel with Parmesan

This is a simple and refreshing vegetable dish that deserves to be better known. The sweet, anise-like flavor of the plant is not to everybody's taste, but to those who do like it, it is quite an addiction.

For this dish, allow a minimum of one large fennel bulb per person. Other ingredients are butter, grated Parmesan cheese, and bread crumbs. Trim the bulbs by slicing off the top stalks, the thick base, and removing all the stringy outer layers of leaves. There is a good deal of waste. Slice the bulbs in half longitudinally. Plunge them into a saucepan of boiling salted water. According to size they should cook for 7 to 10 minutes. When tender enough to be pierced fairly easily with a skewer, drain them.

Have ready a buttered gratin dish or a number of individual dishes. In this arrange the fennel halves, cut-side down. Strew bread crumbs over them (approximately 1 tablespoon per bulb) then grated Parmesan (again, 1 tablespoon per bulb), and finally a few little pieces of butter. Put the gratin dish in a medium oven, 350°F, and leave for 10 to 15 minutes until the cheese and bread crumbs are very pale gold and bubbling.

Oignons à l'étuvée
Onions braised in wine

This is a dish to make when you have a glass of wine: red, white, rosé, sweet, dry, or aromatic (i.e. some sort of Vermouth) to spare and also, perhaps, when you have been bullied or cajoled by one of the Breton onion boys into buying far more onions than you know what to do with. You peel 6 to 8 rather large onions, all the same size. You put them with a tablespoon of olive oil in a thick pan in which they just fit comfortably. You start them off over moderate flame and, when the oil is beginning to sizzle, you pour in a small glass of your wine. Let it boil fiercely a few seconds. Add water to come halfway up the onions. Transfer to a low oven and cook, uncovered, for about 1½ hours. Put back on top of the stove over fast flame for 2 or 3 minutes, until the wine sauce is thick and syrupy. Season. Serve as a separate vegetable, or around a roast.

Serve one onion per person.

Oignons rôtis au four
Roast onions

Medium-size whole onions, unpeeled, are cooked in a baking pan in a slow oven, 340°F, for 1½ to 2 hours. Serve them hot with salt and butter, or cold with a *vinaigrette* dressing.

This is one of the best possible ways of cooking onions in the winter when the oven is, in any case, turned on for the cooking of a stew or some other long-cooked dish. The onions can be served as a first course, or as a separate vegetable after the meat.

Potatoes

It is not until June that English new potatoes become reasonably cheap. The early imported new potatoes never seem to be worth their high price, so in the early part of the summer the old potatoes will have to do. For a change, they are good broiled. Also a potato puree, with the addition of fresh new vegetables or herbs, makes a very good spring soup. The smaller new potatoes are at their best cooked slowly in butter, so that they emerge pale golden outside, melting inside. When they are larger, they make a lovely dish cooked in good stock. Perhaps in this country we eat potatoes so often that very little trouble is taken over their preparation. They repay careful treatment as much as any other vegetable. Because they absorb a good deal of whatever fat they are cooked in, it follows that the fat should always be the best possible; olive oil, butter, pure pork fat, the dripping from a duck, bacon fat, all give their different savors to potatoes. When they are roasted with meat they, as well as the meat, will taste all the better for the flavor of herbs and possibly garlic, which has cooked with the meat. If new potatoes are to be boiled they are best put into boiling water.

Although boiled potatoes are one of the first dishes anybody learns to cook, they always remain a nuisance, as the timing must be accurate, and varies with the quality of the potatoes, so for occasions when there are other dishes to be attended to, or when the meal may be late, it is advisable to learn one or two other simple methods of cooking potatoes, by which they will not suffer if kept waiting for a few minutes. Two such potato dishes are *pommes de terre à la crème* and *pommes de terre fromagées*, for which the recipes are overleaf.

Pommes de terre à la crème
Potatoes with cream

Boil some small whole new potatoes, keeping them rather underdone. Make a cream sauce by heating together 4 tablespoons of butter and ¼ cup of thick fresh cream in a double boiler; stir until thick. Season with salt and ground black pepper. Heat the potatoes in the sauce and season them with a little nutmeg.

Pommes de terre fromagées
New potatoes with Gruyère cheese

Fill a small shallow baking dish with new potatoes, boiled but kept rather undercooked. Pour melted butter over them, then cover them lightly with a mixture of bread crumbs and grated Gruyère cheese. Cook in a moderate oven, 350°F, turning the potatoes around from time to time until they are lightly browned.

Pommes de terre à l'ardennaise
Potatoes with juniper

This is a curious recipe but extremely good if you like the pungent flavor of juniper berries.

Peel 1 pound or so of potatoes and shred them as fine as matches on the fluted blade of a mandolin, or alternatively with a coarse grater. Put them in a strainer or colander and rinse them thoroughly under running cold water to get rid of the starch. Shake them dry in a cloth. Heat 4 tablespoons of butter and a spoonful of olive oil (to prevent the butter burning) in a heavy skillet. Put in your potatoes and let them stew rather than fry in the butter. Add a seasoning of salt, freshly milled pepper, and half a dozen crushed or chopped juniper berries. Turn the potatoes over from time to time. When they have amalgamated into a mass and are quite tender, turn them onto a hot flat dish.

Enough for four.

Pommes fondants

This is the most delicious way of cooking new potatoes. Have them well scraped, washed, and dried. Choose a thick pan, either a small skillet or saucepan or sauté pan of a size which will accommodate the number of potatoes you are going to cook so that each one lies on the bottom of the pan with very little room to spare, or the butter will be wasted and may burn. For 1 pound of potatoes (as much the same size as possible) you need about 3 tablespoons of butter. Melt it very gently in the pan, put the potatoes in whole. Cover the pan and cook over low flame, shaking the pan from time to time to make sure they don't stick. After 10 minutes have a look at them, and when they are getting brown turn them over very carefully and cover the pan again. Small potatoes will take 20 to 25 minutes, larger ones 10 minutes longer. They should be golden on the outside (but not hard like roast potatoes) and melting inside.

Enough for four.

Pommes de terre à la manière d'Apt
Potatoes baked with olives and tomato

3 tablespoons of olive oil, 5 tablespoons of fresh tomato paste, 1 pound of potatoes cut in ¼-inch circles, salt, pepper, a bay leaf, 6 pitted black olives, bread crumbs.

Put the olive oil into a shallow gratin dish, add the tomato paste, the potatoes, salt, pepper, and bay leaf, and simmer for 5 minutes.

Barely cover the potatoes with boiling water, and simmer another 30 minutes. Now add the black olives, and cover with a layer of bread crumbs.

Put in a moderate oven, 350°F, for another 30 minutes. Serve in the same dish.

Enough for four.

Mushrooms cooked in grape leaves

Many people who have a vine growing in their backyards will be glad to know of this excellent dish.

Blanch about a dozen grape leaves in boiling salted water. Drain them and arrange them in a heavy, shallow baking dish which has a well-fitting cover. Pour a film of olive oil over the grape leaves, and fill the pan with cleaned whole flat mushrooms (the great point about this dish is that the grape leaves make cultivated mushrooms taste like portobello mushrooms). Add a little salt and pepper, 3 or 4 whole cloves of garlic, a little more olive oil, and cover the mushrooms with 2 or 3 grape leaves. Put the cover on the dish and cook in a slow oven, 340°F, for about 35 minutes to an hour, according to the size of the mushrooms. Remove the top covering of grape leaves before serving.

NOTE Canned plain grape leaves in natural juices or a very mild brine are sold in many delicatessens, Middle Eastern stores, and some supermarkets. For this dish they do very well. No blanching is necessary. Simply rinse the requisite number under running cold water. The remainder can be stored in the refrigerator for a few days.

Dolmádes
Stuffed grape leaves

A small onion, olive oil, 2 teacups of cooked rice, a few pine nuts, salt, pepper, lemon, stock, a little ground allspice, 3 dozen grape leaves.

Fry the chopped onion in olive oil, mix it with the rice, and add the pine nuts, salt, pepper, spice, and a little olive oil to moisten. If you like, a little chopped lamb can be added, or a chicken liver or two, fried and finely chopped.

Blanch the grape leaves and drain them. Spread them flat on a board, then underside of the leaves uppermost. On each leaf lay about a teaspoon of the rice mixture, roll the leaf up like a sausage, with the ends tucked in, and squeeze each one in the palm of your hand, so that the *dolmádes* will stay rolled up during the cooking. There is no need to tie them. Arrange them in a pan in which they will just fit, in layers. Pour over them enough stock (or water) to come halfway up, cover them with a plate or saucer which fits inside the pan so that the *dolmádes* do not move during the cooking, and simmer them for about ½ hour. Serve cold with lemon juice squeezed over.

Dolmádes can also be served with yogurt or with an egg and lemon sauce (about a teacup of stock with the yolks of 2 eggs and the juice of a lemon whisked over the fire until it is thick and frothy, and poured over the *dolmádes* when cool).

I have often seen it written that *dolmádes* are just as good made with cabbage leaves instead of grape leaves, but it is the taste of the grape leaves and the flavor they give to the stuffing which is so delicious, and which gives them their characteristic Asian flavor.

Enough for six to eight with other small dishes.

Topinambours en daube
Braised Jerusalem artichokes

In a little oil brown a sliced onion, sprinkle in a tablespoon of flour, and stir until golden. Add a small glass of white wine or cider, let it bubble, then put in 1 pound or so of small peeled Jerusalem artichokes, salt, a crushed clove of garlic, a scraping of nutmeg, black pepper, and water just to cover. Simmer until the artichokes are cooked, taking care they don't turn to puree. Before serving stir in a good tablespoon of chopped parsley.

Enough for four.

Topinambours à la provençale
Jerusalem artichokes with tomatoes and herbs

Simmer your artichokes in salted water until they are almost, but not quite, cooked. Strain them. Cut each in two. Heat a little olive oil in a heavy pan, put in the artichokes and, for each 1 pound, add 2 skinned and chopped tomatoes, and a seasoning of dried basil or marjoram chopped with a little scrap of garlic, salt, and freshly milled pepper. By the time the tomatoes have melted to form a sauce, the artichokes should be quite tender and the dish ready to serve, either by itself or as an accompaniment to lamb, pork, or sausages. This is a dish which also goes remarkably well with goose.

1 pound is enough for four.

Carote al marsala
Carrots with marsala

Clean about 1½ pounds of carrots and cut them in half lengthwise, and then in half again. Cut out the woody part in the center, if they are old carrots. Melt 2 tablespoons of butter in a sauté pan and put in the carrots. Turn them over and over so that they become impregnated with the butter. Season with pepper, a little salt, a little sugar, and a minute or two later pour in a small glassful of marsala. Simmer for 5 minutes and then just cover the carrots with water. Put the lid on the pan and stew gently until the carrots are tender. Turn up the flame and let the liquid, which should already be considerably reduced, all but bubble away. The carrots should be shiny, with a little syrupy sauce. Garnish them with a scrap of cut parsley.

Marsala with carrots may sound an unsuitable combination. Try it and see. It is one of my favorite vegetable recipes. Good by itself, or with any kind of lamb.

Enough for four or five.

Navets glacés
Glazed turnips

Put small, whole, peeled turnips (as nearly as possible the same size) into boiling salted water and cook them for 10 to 15 minutes, until they are nearly ready. Drain them, setting aside a little of the water. Put them into a small buttered dish which will bear the heat of the flame, sprinkle them with superfine sugar, put more butter on the top, and 2 or 3 tablespoons of the water in which they have cooked, and put the dish on very low fire until the sauce turns brown and slightly sticky. Watch carefully to see that it doesn't burn. Spoon a little of the glaze over each turnip and serve as they are, in the same dish.

Carrots stewed with rice

A Turkish dish.

Clean 1 pound of young carrots and cut in halves lengthwise. Cover the bottom of a thick pan with oil; when it has warmed put in the carrots and let them get thoroughly impregnated with the oil; add 2 tablespoons of rice, and stir it around with the carrots; just cover carrots and rice with water, add a little salt. Simmer for about 25 minutes until the carrots and rice are cooked and most of the liquid evaporated; stir in a handful of chopped parsley and mint.

Serve cold, in their liquid, which will be quite thick, with a squeeze of lemon juice.

Enough for four to five.

Tomates provençales
Provençal tomatoes

Cut large ripe tomatoes in half. With a small knife make several incisions crosswise in the pulp of the tomatoes, and in these rub salt, pepper, and crushed garlic. Chop finely a good handful of parsley and spread each half tomato with it, pressing it well in.

Pour a few drops of olive oil on each and cook under the broiler for preference, or in a hot oven, 400°F.

To be quite perfect, *tomates provençales* should be slightly blackened on the cut surface.

Pipérade

1 pound of onions, 3 fairly large sweet red bell peppers or about 6 of the small green ones, in season in the Basque country long before the red ones, 1 pound of tomatoes, salt, pepper, marjoram, 6 eggs.

In a heavy skillet or sauté pan heat a little olive oil, put in the sliced onions, and let them cook slowly, turning golden but not brown; then put in the peppers, cut into strips; let this cook until it is soft, then add the chopped tomatoes, with a seasoning of salt, ground black pepper, and a little marjoram. Cook with the cover on the pan.

When the whole mixture has become almost the consistency of a puree, pour in the beaten eggs, and stir gently, exactly as for ordinary scrambled eggs. Take care not to let them get overcooked.

Enough for five to six.

Spinach and eggs

Clean 1 pound of spinach very carefully and drain it well. Cook it, without water, for about 5 minutes, adding a little salt. Squeeze the water out of it, put it into a fireproof dish in which a good lump of butter has been melted; heat it very gently in the oven. When it is hot, add 2 or 3 tablespoons of boiled cream and 2 sliced hard-boiled eggs and cook for another minute or two.

Serve very hot, as a separate vegetable course. 1 pound of spinach is enough for two people.

SALADS

Sweet pepper and watercress salad

1 large fleshy red bell pepper, 1 shallot, a half bunch of watercress.

Cut the stalk end from the pepper, remove the seeds, then rinse the pepper in cold water to ensure that not one seed is lurking. Slice the pepper into strips. Mix these with the shallot peeled and sliced paper thin.

Rinse the watercress, discard the muddy and ragged part of the stalks, cut the rest with scissors into rather large pieces.

The dressing should be made with salt, a scrap of sugar, olive oil, lemon juice, or mild wine vinegar. A good salad to offer with veal scallops or pork chops.

Enough for two to three.

Pepper salad

Broil the peppers until the skins turn black and will flake off. This takes about 20 minutes under a broiler, the peppers being turned as soon as one side is done. When they have cooled a little, peel off the skin, take out the seeds, wash the peppers under the cold faucet, cut them into strips, and dress with olive oil, lemon juice, chopped garlic, and parsley.

Tomato salad

Slice the tomatoes into thick circles and arrange them on a large flat dish. Season with ground black pepper, and strew over them plenty of chopped fresh herbs, tarragon, chives, basil, parsley, whatever is available, and a little garlic. Just before serving sprinkle with salt and olive oil. Made in this way a tomato salad is fresh and crisp and aromatic; it is the salting and dressing of tomatoes several hours before they are to be served which makes them watery and clammy, although it has to be admitted that all the precautions in the world can do little to make commercially grown English and Channel Island tomatoes anything but mushy and tasteless.

Leaf Salads

Anyone who has visited Venice in the spring and in the early fall will remember the ravishing and original salads offered in the Venetian restaurants, and the tremendous display of salad greens and green stuff to be seen on the stalls in the Rialto market.

Many of these salad stuffs are quite unfamiliar to English eyes. There are three or four varieties of chicory leaves, none of these resembling what we know by that name. One of the northern Italian *cicoria* varieties is the rose-red plant known as *cicoria spadona* or sword-leaved chicory, a fourth is a lettuce-like plant and, just to help, all these chicories are also called *radicchio*; this is not to be confused with radish or *ravanelli*, of which the leaves are also eaten in salad.

Some of the salad plants, notably the beautiful rose-red chicory, have a more decorative value than taste; the green ones are mild and slightly bitter; another, more interesting, salad leaf is *rugeta* or in Venice, *rucola* (nearly all Venetian food names whether fish, fungi, or vegetable, differ from those of the rest of Italy), which has a peppery little leaf once familiar in England as arugula, in France as *roquette*, in Greece it is *rocca*, and in Germany *senfkohl* which means mustard herb; then there is corn salad or lamb's lettuce (in Venetian, *gallinelle*, in French *mâche*), and little bright-green serrated leaves which the market women call *salatina*.

In the market, all these salad furnishings are offered for sale in separate boxes, each variety lightly piled up, shining and clean, ready for weighing out. (In Italy salads are bought by the kilo (2¼ pounds), not by the piece.) There will also be boxes of crisp fennel, violet-leaved artichokes and intensely green zucchini, their bright marigold-colored flowers still intact.

In the restaurants, the true Venetian restaurants that is, rather than the hotel dining rooms where you may well have to put up with English-type lettuce and tomato dressed with overrefined olive oil, you will see big bowls of mixed leaves arranged like full-blown peonies for a table decoration, infinitely fresh and appetizing. (It is an interesting point that while few Italians are capable of making a graceful flower arrangement, their foodstuffs are invariably displayed with subtle artistry.) When you order a salad, a waiter will bring one of these bowls to your table so that you can make your choice. Your salad will be mixed for you; the dressing will be of fruity olive oil which has character (it is rare in northern Italy to find poor olive oil) and, in the Veneto, a very good pale rosé wine vinegar. In short you will get a civilized salad which is a treat to the eye as well as a stimulus to the palate and a refreshment to the spirit.

In the early summer of 1969 the salads of Venice made such an impact on one of my sisters—it was her first visit to Venice —that we went to the market and bought seeds of all the local salad plants that we could find.

Some of these plants, notably the arugula (its Latin name is *Eruca sativa*; it used to be common in English gardens) did remarkably well that summer in my sister's little cottage garden, near Petersfield; in another garden on the Isle of Wight it grew like a weed, far into the fall. Sorrel and corn salad, single-leaved parsley, and pink chicory were all forthcoming from these gardens, and so it was that during the warm summer and the long miraculous fall of that year we all feasted on fresh and spring-like salads almost every day of our lives. English radishes were uncommonly crisp and good, English fava beans scented the greengrocers' stores like a beanfield, snow peas were so delicate and sweet that to eat them raw was like tasting some extraordinary new kind of sorbet and there were those heartening salads, not it is true at all like the Venetian salads but delicious in their own way, and original. (In Venice, we could not have eaten them all summer through. It is too hot. The leafy little salads vanish by the end of May, to reappear again only in the fall.)

Angevin salad

Hearts of 2 lettuces or of 2 curly endives (also called chicory) or Batavian endives, ½ pound of Gruyère or Emmental cheese, olive oil, and wine vinegar for the dressing.

Salad and cheese in one course—not American but French, and very delicate and unusual. The salad must be fresh and crisp. Wash and dry it well ahead of time. With it in the bowl mix the Gruyère or Emmental (the latter is the one with the large holes, whereas the real Gruyère has very small ones) cut into tiny cubes. Add the dressing, made from 6 tablespoons of olive oil to a teaspoon or two at most of vinegar, at the last minute.

Instead of olive oil, the light walnut oil of Touraine can be used for the dressing. Combined with the cheese it makes a beautiful and interesting mixture.

This is a lovely salad to serve after a roast turkey or capon. Enough for four.

Lentil salad

Stewed lentils, lentil soup, lentils and bacon are filling winter dishes. They also make a first-class salad for the early summer, before the lettuces and new vegetables have started; the flavor of good olive oil combined with lentils is excellent.

Pick over 1–1¼ cups of brown lentils, and rinse in cold water. Cook the lentils, covered with fresh water, for 20 to 25 minutes, until just done. Add salt toward the end of the cooking time. Strain them, stir in a few finely cut circles of raw onion and plenty of olive oil. See that the seasoning is right and when the salad is cold garnish it with quarters of hard-boiled egg.

Enough for four.

Endive and beet salad

1 pound of Belgian endives or chicory, olive oil, salt, freshly milled pepper, lemon juice, 2 medium-size cooked beets, tarragon vinegar.

Discard the outside leaves of the endives; cut off the root ends, using a stainless-steel or silver knife; wipe the endives clean with a soft cloth. Cut them across into ½-inch chunks. Put the prepared endives in a bowl. Mix them with a dressing of olive oil, salt, freshly milled pepper, and lemon juice.

Prepare the beets separately. Peel them, dice them, season with plenty of salt, freshly milled pepper, and a dressing of oil and a very little tarragon vinegar. At the last moment, put the beet in the salad bowl in the center of the endives.

Enough for four.

Cucumber and chive salad

A cucumber, salt and pepper, a teaspoon of sugar, a teaspoon of tarragon vinegar, a small cup of cream, olive oil, a few chives.

Slice the pared cucumber paper thin (on a mandolin or *coupe-julienne*, this is a matter of less than a minute). Sprinkle coarse salt over the cucumber and let it drain in a colander for half an hour. If necessary, rinse them to get rid of excess salt. Drain them well.

Mix the sugar and vinegar together, then add the cream, pepper, and salt. Add about 2 tablespoons of olive oil and the chopped chives, and pour the dressing over the cucumber in a shallow dish.

A plain cucumber salad with no dressing at all other than a few drops each of olive oil and tarragon vinegar is equally delicious.

Enough for three to four.

Rice and cucumber salad

Put 2½ cups of good-quality rice in a 6.2-quart capacity saucepan nearly full of boiling salted water. Add half a lemon and when the water comes back to a boil float a couple of tablespoons of oil on the top. This will help prevent the water boiling over. The rice will be cooked in 12 to 18 minutes, depending upon the type of rice you are using. In any case, keep it on the firm side.

As soon as you have drained the rice in a colander, turn it into a big bowl. Immediately, add any necessary salt, approximately 6 tablespoons of oil, 2 teaspoons of tarragon vinegar, 2 shallots sliced into paper-thin circles, and a good quantity of grated nutmeg. This latter seasoning makes the whole difference.

Have ready a cucumber, peeled and sliced in four lengthwise, the seeds removed, the flesh cut into small cubes, and seasoned with salt. Mix these with the rice. Add also, if you like, a dozen or so black olives, a few cubes of raw celery, and a few shreds of raw red or green bell pepper. Mix all together very lightly and the salad is ready, except for a sprinkling of chives or parsley.

As a change from cucumber, try instead little cubes of green or yellow honeydew melon. This salad makes a good accompaniment to cold turkey and chicken.

Enough for six to eight.

Insalata di finocchi e cetrioli
Salad of fennel and cucumber

Cut half an unpeeled cucumber into slices ¼ inch thick, then cut each slice into 4 small squares. Slice a bulb of fennel into thin strips, cut 3 or 4 radishes into slices, and mix with the cucumber. Add a little chopped mint and season with salt, pepper, garlic, olive oil, and lemon juice. Before serving add 2 quartered hard-boiled eggs.

The addition of an orange cut into segments makes this an excellent salad to serve with duck or game.

Enough for two to three.

Orange and celery salad	Short pieces of celery and quarters of orange, with a very little dressing of oil and lemon. Especially good to accompany a terrine.

Spiced rice salad	*1–1¼ cups rice, a piece of fresh ginger or dried gingerroot, black pepper, nutmeg, coriander seeds, lemon, a shallot, olive oil, a handful of mixed raisins and currants, 3 or 4 fresh or dried apricots, almonds, or pine nuts.*

Boil the rice with the ginger in salted water for 14 to 15 minutes; drain very carefully; remove the ginger; while still warm season the rice with black pepper, grated nutmeg, half a teaspoon of pounded coriander seeds, a little lemon juice, and the shallot cut into fine circles; stir in enough olive oil to make the rice moist but not mushy, then add the raisins and currants, previously simmered a few minutes in water to make them swell, then drained, and the apricots, raw, if fresh ones are being used, soaked, and lightly cooked if they are dried.

Garnish with roasted almonds or pine nuts.

Enough for three to four.

Céléri-rave rémoulade

To make this celery root hors-d'oeuvre—a dish familiar to anyone who has eaten regularly in the smaller restaurants of Paris and the French provinces—you really do need to be in possession of that invaluable utensil known as a mandolin. On the fluted blade of the mandolin shred the peeled celery root into thin stick pieces or use a julienne blade in a food processor. As you proceed, put all into a bowl of cold water acidulated with lemon juice or vinegar. Bring a big saucepan of water, also acidulated, and salted, to a boil. Plunge the drained celery root into it. Leave it until the water comes back to a boil again, no longer, then drain it as dry as you can, in a colander. This brief blanching makes all the difference to a celery root salad, for in its totally raw state many people find it hard to digest. Also, after blanching, it absorbs less dressing or mayonnaise.

When the celery root has cooled, mix it with a very stiff homemade mayonnaise very strongly flavored with mustard. Pile the celery root onto a shallow dish, sprinkle it with parsley, and serve it fairly quickly; if left to stand for any length of time it begins to look rather unattractive and messy.

An average-size celery root, weighing approximately 1 pound, plus about generous ¾ cup of mayonnaise (2 egg yolks) will make an ample hors-d'oeuvre for four.

Coriander mushrooms

This is a quickly cooked little dish which makes a delicious cold hors-d'oeuvre. The aromatics used are similar to those which go into the well-known *champignons à la grecque*, but the method is simpler, and the result even better.

Ingredients are: 6 ounces of firm, white, round, and very fresh mushrooms, lemon juice, 2 tablespoons of olive oil, a teaspoon of coriander seeds, one or two bay leaves, salt, freshly milled pepper.

Rinse the mushrooms, wipe them dry with a clean cloth, slice them (but do not peel them) into quarters, or if they are large into eighths. The stalks should be neatly trimmed. Squeeze over them a little lemon juice.

In a heavy skillet or sauté pan, warm the olive oil. Into it put the coriander seeds, which should be already crushed in a mortar. Let them heat for a few seconds. Keep the heat low. Put in the mushrooms and the bay leaves. Add the seasoning. Let the mushrooms cook gently for a minute, cover the pan, and leave them, still over very low heat, for another 3 to 5 minutes.

Uncover the pan. Decant the mushrooms—with all their juices—into a shallow serving dish and sprinkle them with fresh olive oil and lemon juice.

Whether the mushrooms are to be served hot or cold do not forget to put the bay leaf, which has cooked with them, into the serving dish. The combined scents of coriander and bay go to make up part of the true essence of the dish. And it is important to note that cultivated mushrooms should not be cooked for longer than the time specified.

In larger quantities the same dish can be made as a hot vegetable to be eaten with veal or chicken.

Cooked mushrooms do not keep well, but a day or two in the refrigerator does not harm this coriander-spiced dish. It is also worth remembering that uncooked cultivated mushrooms can be stored in a plastic box in the refrigerator and will keep fresh for a couple of days.

Enough for three.

PASTA, GNOCCHI & POLENTA

The cooking and serving of pasta

In Italy the amount of pasta allowed for each person is 3–4 ounces, whether homemade or dried. The latter is usually cooked in a large quantity of boiling salted water. It should be cooked *al dente*—that is, very slightly resistant—and it should be strained without delay.

A warmed serving dish should be ready, and the pasta should be eaten as soon as it has been prepared.

An alternative, but little-known, way of cooking manufactured pasta is to calculate 4 cups of water to every ¼ pound of dried pasta. Bring the water to a boil; add a tablespoon of salt for every 1.8 quarts of water and add the pasta. After it comes back to a boil let it continue boiling for 3 minutes. Turn off the heat, cover the saucepan with a towel and the lid, leave it for 5 to 8 minutes, according to the thickness of the pasta, e.g. 5 minutes for *spaghettini*, 8 for *maccheroni rigati,* which are short tubes, ridged and thick. At the end of this time the pasta should be *al dente*.

I learned this excellent method from the directions given on a package of Agnesi pasta bought in the early 1970s. I find it infinitely more preferable to the old-fashioned way.

The addition of a generous lump of butter left to melt on the top of the pasta as it is served, or of a little olive oil put into the heated dish before the cooked pasta is turned into it, are both valuable improvements. Whether the sauce is served separately or stirred into the pasta is a matter of taste.

Spaghetti all'olio e aglio

Spaghetti with oil and garlic

Pasta is often eaten in Italy with no embellishment but oil and garlic. Those who are particularly addicted to garlic and spaghetti will find this dish excellent, others will probably abominate it. It is essential that the oil be olive oil and of good quality.

When your spaghetti is cooked, barely warm a cup of oil in a small pan, and into it stir whatever quantity of finely chopped garlic you fancy. Let it soak in the oil a bare minute, without frying, then stir the whole mixture into the spaghetti. You can add chopped parsley or any other herb, and of course grated cheese if you wish, although the Neapolitans do not serve cheese with spaghetti cooked in this way. If you like the taste of garlic without actually wishing to eat the bulb itself, pour the oil onto the spaghetti through a strainer, leaving the chopped garlic behind.

Spaghetti all'olio e aglio e saetini

Spaghetti with oil, garlic, and chile

Cook the spaghetti in the usual way, put it into a hot dish, and pour over it a generous amount of very hot olive oil in which have been fried several coarsely chopped cloves of garlic and some red pepper flakes.

Salsa alla marinara

When pasta is served with a sauce based on a certain quantity of olive oil it is not always considered necessary to serve cheese as well. Some Italians, indeed, consider it absurd to mix cheese and oil; either ingredient, they say, provides, with the pasta, sufficient nourishment to make a balanced dish.

To make the marinara sauce, heat 4 or 5 tablespoons of olive oil in a skillet. When it is hot but not smoking, throw in several sliced cloves of garlic; after a few seconds add 1½ pounds of ripe skinned tomatoes, roughly chopped. Let them cook about 3 minutes only. Season with salt and pepper, and then add a few coarsely chopped leaves of fresh basil, or failing that, some parsley. The sauce is now ready to be served with your pasta, or for that matter, with boiled rice or haricot beans. The amount of garlic used is entirely a matter of taste, and those who like only a faint flavor can remove it from the pan before putting in the tomatoes, for it will already have scented the oil.

Enough sauce for four to five.

Salsa di pomidoro crudo
Sauce of raw tomatoes

Plunge 1 pound of very ripe tomatoes into boiling water and skin them. Chop them up, adding a little finely cut onion, garlic, parsley, or fresh basil, and as much good olive oil as you care for. Make it an hour or two before it is to be served.

Sauce of dried cèpes

Take 2–3 ounces of dried cèpes. Soak the cèpes in enough warm water to cover them for 20 minutes. Transfer the cèpes and the liquid to a small pan, add salt and pepper, and simmer for 30 minutes. Strain them, keeping the water they have cooked in, which you strain again through a cheesecloth. Put this back in the pan, and melt 4–6 tablespoons of butter in it. Serve the sauce and the cèpes over spaghetti.

Pesto

1 large bunch of fresh basil, garlic, scant ¼–generous ¼ cup pine nuts, ¼–generous ⅓ cup grated Sardo *or Parmesan cheese, 3–4 tablespoons of olive oil.*

Pound the basil leaves (there should be about 2 ounces when the stalks have been removed) in a mortar with 1 or 2 cloves of garlic, a little salt, and the pine nuts. Add the cheese. (*Sardo* is the pungent Sardinian ewe's milk cheese which is exported in large quantities to Genoa to make pesto. Parmesan and *Sardo* are sometimes used in equal quantities, or all Parmesan, which gives the pesto a milder flavor.)

When the pesto is a thick puree, start adding the olive oil, a little at a time. Stir it steadily and see that it is amalgamating with the other ingredients, as the finished sauce should have the consistency of creamed butter. If made in larger quantities pesto may be stored in jars, covered with a layer of olive oil.

This is the famous sauce which is eaten by the Genoese with all kinds of pasta, with gnocchi (see Potato Gnocchi p113), and as a flavoring for soups. The Genoese claim that their basil has a far superior flavor to that grown in other parts of Italy, and assert that a good pesto can only be made with Genoese basil. As made in Genoa it is certainly one of the best sauces yet invented for pasta, and 1 tablespoon of pesto stirred in at the last minute gives a most delicious flavor to a minestrone (see Minestrone, p10 and La soupe au pistou, p14). Try it also with baked potatoes instead of butter.

You can make a versions of this sauce with parsley instead of basil, and walnuts can be used instead of pine nuts.

Enough sauce for four to five.

Spaghetti con salsa di zucchini

Spaghetti with zucchini

Cut a good quantity (about 1½ pounds) of small unpeeled zucchini into thin circles. Sprinkle them with salt and put them in a colander so that the water drains away.

Fry them gently in oil or butter, or a mixture of the two, and when they are soft pour them over the dish of spaghetti or any other pasta.

A way of serving spaghetti which I believe is popular in the south, particularly in Positano.

Enough sauce for four.

Tonnellini con funghi e piselli

Tonnellini with mushrooms and green peas

Tonnellini are very fine, match-like noodles, homemade with fresh egg pasta dough. This can also be made with spaghetti. The sauce consists of ½ pound of mushrooms cut into thin slices, an onion, and 1 pound of green peas. Cook the green peas in butter with the finely chopped onion, adding a very little water. After 10 minutes add the mushrooms. When the peas and mushrooms are cooked, pour them over the prepared pasta, and serve cheese separately.

Enough sauce for four.

Tortelli di erbette

These *tortelli*, a kind of ravioli, are one of the summer specialties of the province of Parma, where a number of original dishes are to be found. The filling is made with the green leaves of young beets, spinach beet, or chard. For the pasta, for six people, pour generous 1¾ cups of flour in a mound onto a pastry board. Make a hole in the center and into it break 3 or 4 eggs and a teaspoon of salt. Fold the flour over the eggs (without the addition of water) and knead until you have a soft dough. Divide this into 2 or 4 pieces. Roll each piece out, and stretch it by putting it through a pasta machine, reducing the thickness each time, until it is very thin and you can pick it up like a piece of fine material. If you don't have a pasta machine, roll the pasta out and wrap it around the rolling pin, Roll again and wrap around the rolling pin again, stretching it a little more each time. Sprinkle flour over it each time so that it doesn't stick.

For the filling puree 6 ounces of cooked spinach, thoroughly drained, whiz in a food processor or put through a food mill, and mix it with the same quantity of cream cheese (ricotta as used in Parma), ¼ cup of grated Parmesan, salt, pepper, a liberal grating of nutmeg, and 2 eggs.

Cut the prepared pasta into pieces about 2 x 2½ inches, if possible with a cutter which has scalloped edges. Onto half the squares put small spoonfuls of the spinach mixture. Cover them with the other squares and press down the edges, moistening them a little so that they are well closed. Cook them in plenty of boiling salted water for 4 or 5 minutes, until they rise to the top. Serve them in a heated dish with melted butter and plenty of grated Parmesan poured over.

Enough for six.

Chiocciole al mascarpone e noce

Pasta shells with cream cheese and walnuts

Boil 6–8 ounces of pasta shells. Some are very hard, and take as long as 20 minutes, and although they are small they need just as large a proportion of water for the cooking as other factory-made pasta.

The sauce is prepared as follows: in a fireproof serving dish melt a lump of butter, and for 3 people ½–¾ cup of mascarpone or other heavy-cream cheese. It must just gently heat, not boil. Into this mixture put your cooked and drained pasta. Turn it around and around adding two or three spoonfuls of grated Parmesan. Add scant ½ cup or so (shell weight) of roughly chopped walnuts. Serve more grated cheese separately.

This is an exquisite dish when well prepared, but it is filling and rich, so a little goes a long way.

Enough for three people.

Tuoni e lampo

Thunder and lightning

A peasant recipe given to me by the Caprese writer Edwin Cerio. When the bottom of a sack of pasta is reached, there are always broken pieces, which are sold cheaply, by 2¼ pounds—all shapes and sizes of pasta mixed together. It is partly these broken pieces which constitute the charm of the dish, particularly for the children, who enjoy finding the different shapes on their plates. They are mixed with *ceci*, or chickpeas, in about equal quantities. The chickpeas, say scant 1½ cups, must be soaked overnight, covered with water, and cooked slowly for 2 to 3 hours. When they are all but ready, cook the pasta separately in boiling salted water; drain it and add it to the chickpeas, which should by this time have absorbed most of their liquid. Stir grated Parmesan into the dish and serve it with butter, or oil, or tomato sauce (p98). The nutty flavor and the slightly hard texture of the chickpeas make a pleasant contrast to the softness of the pasta.

Enough for three to four.

NOTE: Canned chickpeas can be used in this recipe if you prefer.

Ravioli caprese

Capri ravioli

This recipe was one used by Antonio, who cooked for Norman Douglas. Edwin Cerio, the Caprese writer, told me that the only herb in the filling should be marjoram, and that to put basil as well was a "foreign habit." Slightly differing versions of the cheese stuffing are made in other parts of Italy.

For the pasta, mix 4 tablespoons of butter with generous 1¾ cups of flour. Add salt and enough boiling water (approximately a cupful) to make a stiff dough. Knead it a little, divide it into two parts, and roll each one out on a floured board. This is a very easy pasta to work, and takes less time than the pasta made with eggs. It is quickly rolled out very thin and need not be stretched, but you can put it through a pasta machine a few times if you prefer. If you have not a sufficiently large board, divide the dough into four parts, as it is impossible to get the sheets of pasta thin enough if space on the board is inadequate.

When making this or any other pasta, remember to have a clean cloth or towel ready on a table or dresser on which to lay the ready-prepared sheets of pasta; while the rest are being rolled out, cover them with another cloth or they will, even in a short time, become crusty, which will cause the pasta to break when the filling and cutting out of the ravioli is to be done. Remember also to have a bowl of flour to hand; the surface of the pasta must be repeatedly sprinkled with flour while it is being rolled out to prevent it from sticking; turn it over fairly often so that both sides are well floured.

Pasta for ravioli should be as thin as is consistent with it remaining intact and not tearing during the filling and cutting-out process. Having made the pasta once or twice, knowledge of the right manageable thickness comes automatically.

Lastly, do not forget the salt.

For the filling mix together generous 1 cup of grated Parmesan and 6 ounces of *caciotta* (a sheep's milk cheese made both in Tuscany and in the south; there is a local one made in Capri from goat milk—in England use *provolone* or Gruyère). Add a cupful of milk, 3 eggs, pepper, nutmeg, and either basil or marjoram or both.

When the two sheets of pasta are ready, put little mounds (about a teaspoonful) of the cheese mixture at regular intervals, about 1½ inches apart, on one of them. Cover with the second sheet of pasta, letting it lie loosely, not stretched over the stuffing. With a round cutter, about 1½ inches in diameter, separate each of the ravioli. See that the edges are well closed, but it should not be necessary with this pasta to brush them with egg. Put the prepared ravioli onto a floured board or dish, in one layer only. Cover them with a floured cloth until it is time to cook them. They will keep a day or so, if necessary. Slide them into gently boiling salted water, and cook them for about 4 minutes, until they rise to the top. Lift them out carefully with a perforated spoon, put them in a heated dish, and pour some melted butter and grated cheese over them. Serve more cheese separately.

A few of these cheese ravioli cooked and served in a chicken or meat broth make a delicious soup.

Ravioli made with this pasta also make excellent little hot pasties. Instead of cooking them in water, fry them in very hot dripping or oil for about half a minute on each side, lift them from the pan with a perforated spoon, and serve them at once as the cheese filling is just about to melt. Good to serve with drinks.

Enough for six.

Gnocchi verdi

Green gnocchi

12 ounces of cooked and chopped spinach (i.e. 1 pound to start with), salt, pepper, nutmeg, a little butter, generous 1 cup of ricotta, 2 eggs, generous ⅓ cup of grated Parmesan, 3 tablespoons of flour, and for the sauce plenty of melted butter and grated Parmesan.

Cook the cleaned spinach with a little salt but no water. Drain it, press it absolutely dry, then chop it finely. Put it into a pan with the salt, pepper, nutmeg, a nut of butter, and the mashed ricotta. Stir all the ingredients together over low flame for 5 minutes. Remove the pan from the fire and beat in the eggs, the grated Parmesan, and the flour. Leave the mixture in the refrigerator for several hours, or better still, overnight.

Spread a pastry board with flour, form little croquettes about the size of a cork with the spinach mixture, roll them in the flour, and when they are all ready drop them carefully into a large pan of barely simmering, slightly salted water.

(Do not be alarmed if the mixture seems rather soft; the eggs and the flour hold the gnocchi together as soon as they are put into the boiling water.)

Either the gnocchi must be cooked in a very large saucepan or else the operation must be carried out in two or three relays, as there must be plenty of room for them in the pan. When they rise to the top, which will be in 5 to 8 minutes, they are ready. They will disintegrate if left too long. Take them out with a perforated draining spoon, drain them carefully in a colander or strainer, and when the first batch is ready slide them into a shallow fireproof dish already prepared with 2 tablespoons of melted butter and a thin layer of grated Parmesan cheese. Put the dish in the oven to keep hot while the rest of the gnocchi are cooked. When all are done, put another 2 tablespoons of butter and a generous amount of cheese over them and leave the dish in the oven for 5 minutes.

This quantity is sufficient for four people for a first course.

Gnocchi di patate

Potato gnocchi

2 pounds of potatoes, generous 1¾ cups of flour, 2 tablespoons of butter, 2 eggs, salt, pepper.

Make a puree of the cooked potatoes, as dry as possible. Mix in the flour, the butter, and the eggs. Season with salt and pepper and knead to a dough.

Roll it into long sausage-like rolls the thickness of a finger. Cut into pieces about ¾ inches long, and in each of these little cylinders make a dent with the finger, lengthwise, so that they become almost crescent-shaped, like a curl of butter. Drop them one by one into a large pan of gently boiling salted water and cook them for about 3 minutes. When they float to the top they are done. Take them out of the pan with a perforated spoon and put them into a heated fireproof dish with butter and grated cheese. Leave them a minute or two in a warm oven, and serve them either plain or in the Genoese way with pesto (p100), or with a meat *sugo*.

Enough for four.

Polenta

Cornmeal, yellow maize flour, is one of the staple foods of northern Italy, particularly of Lombardy and the Veneto, where boiled cornmeal very often takes the place of bread. There are different qualities of this *farina gialla*, coarsely or finely ground. Plainly boiled cornmeal is dull and rather stodgy, but left to get cold and then fried in oil, toasted on the broiler, or baked in the oven, with meat or tomato sauce or with butter and cheese, it can be very good. In the Veneto it is the inevitable accompaniment to little roasted birds, and to *baccalà*. It can be made into gnocchi; into a kind of fried sandwich containing cheese and ham; and into a filling winter *pasticciata*, with a cheese sauce and white truffles.

To cook cornmeal, boil about 1.3 quarts of salted water in a fairly large saucepan. Pour in scant 3¼ cups of finely ground cornmeal (enough for at least 10 people). Stir it around with a wooden spoon until it is a thick, smooth mass. Now let it cook very slowly, stirring frequently, for 20 minutes. See that there is enough salt. Turn the cornmeal out onto a large platter, or wooden board, or marble slab. It can be eaten at once with butter and cheese, or with a meat or tomato sauce, with boiled broccoli or with roasted quails or other little birds on the top; or it can be left until cold, cut into squares or circles and cooked in any of the ways already mentioned.

For coarsely ground cornmeal use a little more water for the initial cooking.

NOTE: Quick-cooking cornmeal (Valsugana and other Italian brands are widely available) can be cooked in about 8 minutes.

Polenta grassa
Rich polenta

Cook the cornmeal as already described and have ready a buttered fireproof dish. Spread it with a layer of cornmeal, and on this put slices of *fontina*, the rich, buttery cheese of Piedmont, and small pieces of butter; then another layer of cornmeal, and more cheese and butter. Cook in the oven or under the broiler until the top is browned.

Polenta pasticciata
Polenta pie

A Milanese dish. Cook generous 1½ cups of fine cornmeal in 3½ cups of water, as already described, and let it cool. In the meantime prepare a béchamel sauce with 3–4 tablespoons of butter, 2 tablespoons of flour, and scant 3¼ cups of warmed milk. Season with salt, pepper, and nutmeg. When the sauce has cooked for a good 15 minutes, stir in generous ⅓ cup of grated cheese.

Wash ½ pound of mushrooms and cut them into fine slices. Cook them for 3 or 4 minutes in a little butter. (In Milan white truffles are used, when in season; which is one way of turning a peasant dish into a rich man's feast.) Butter a wide, shallow cake pan or fireproof dish. On top of the layer of cornmeal spread some of the béchamel, then some of the mushrooms. Two more layers of cornmeal, mushrooms, and béchamel, and on top of the béchamel spread generous ¼ cup of grated Parmesan or Gruyère. Bake in a fairly hot oven for about 30 minutes until there is a bubbling golden crust on the top of the dish. Serve as it is.

Enough for six to eight people.

Trufflesville Regis

On Saturday morning the entire main shopping thoroughfare of the Piedmontese market town of Alba in the Italian province of Cuneo is closed to traffic. The stalls are set up in the middle of the street, and the awnings stretch right across it from sidewalk to sidewalk. Coming from the big Piazza Savona you pass first stall upon stall of clothes, bales of cloth, household wares, plastics and, on the ground, huge copper polenta pots. The vegetable, fruit, and cheese stalls fill the vast piazza at the far end of the street and ramble right around and to the back of the great red *duomo*. (There are some very remarkable carved and inlaid choir stalls in Alba's cathedral. The artist, Bernardo Cidonio, has created magnificent fruitwood panels showing the local landscapes, castles, and towers, architectural vistas, and still-lifes of the fruit and even of the cooking pots of the region. These treasures, dating from 1501, unheralded by guidebooks, shouldn't be missed.)

At this season in Alba there are beautiful pears and apples, and especially interesting red and yellow bell peppers, in shape rather like the outsize squashy tomatoes of Provence, very fleshy and sweet, a specialty of the neighborhood. What we have really come to Alba to see and eat, though, are white truffles, and these are to be found in the poultry, egg, and mushroom market held in yet another enormous piazza (Alba seems to be all piazzas, churches, red towers, and white truffles), and will not start, they say, until nine-thirty. In the meantime there are baskets of prime mushrooms to look at and to smell, chestnut and ocher-colored *funghi porcini*, the cèpes or *Boletus edulis* common in the wooded country of Piedmont, where everything possible is kingly, the *Amanita caesari* are *funghi reali*, royal mushrooms. They are the *oronges* considered by some French fungi-fanciers, as well as by the Piedmontese to be the best of all mushrooms.

In Piedmont the royal mushroom is most commonly eaten as an hors-d'œuvre, sliced raw and very fine, prepared only when you order it. Since few Piedmontese restaurateurs supply printed menus, expecting their clients to be familiar with the specialties, it is well for tourists to know that they won't get fungi unless they ask for them. The basket will then be brought to your table, you pick out the ones you fancy, making as much fuss as possible about the freshness and size, instruct the waiter as to their preparation (*funghi porcini* are best broiled), and they are charged according to weight.

As far as the beautiful salad of tangerine-bordered, white-and-cream cross-sections of *funghi reali* is concerned, normally it is seasoned only with salt, olive oil, and lemon juice, but at this season you have to be pretty quick off the mark to prevent the Piedmontese in general and the Albesi in particular from destroying this exquisite and delicate mushroom with a shower of *tartufi bianchi*.

It is not that the white truffles, which are not white but putty-colored, are not entirely marvelous and extraordinary. It is simply that their scent is so overpowering and all-penetrating that nothing delicate can stand up to their assault. The one creation evolved by the Piedmontese that accords perfectly with the white truffle is the famous *fonduta*, a dish made from the fat, rich Val d'Aosta cheese called *fontina*, cut into cubes and steeped in milk for an essential minimum of 12 hours, then cooked, by those very few who have the knack, to a velvety, egg-thickened cream with an appearance entirely guileless until the rain of truffles, sliced raw in flake-fine slivers with a special type of *mandoline-*

cutter, descends upon it. There is something about *fontina* cheese, a hint of corruption and decadence in its flavor, that gives it a true affinity with the rootless, mysterious tuber dug up out of the ground.

The black truffles (*Tuber melanosporum*) of Périgord are, traditionally, sniffed out by pigs. In Provence and the Languedoc, dogs are trained to locate and indicate the presence of truffles by scratching the patches of ground that conceal them. In Piedmont the white truffle (*Tuber magnatum*) is located in the same way. In the village of Roddi, not far from Alba, there is a training establishment for truffle hounds. Most of the dogs are mongrels. Valuable property, these Bobbis and Fidos, to the farmers and peasants who go about their truffle-digging secretively by dawn light, bearing their little hatchets for extracting the treasure from the earth. No system of truffle cultivation in the technical sense has ever yet been evolved, but according to Professor Gagliardi and Doctor Persiani in their Italian book on mushrooms and truffles, truffles can be and are propagated successfully by the reburying of mature truffles and spores close to the collateral roots of oaks and beeches, and in chalky ground with a southerly aspect. In five to 10 years the chosen area may or may not yield a truffle harvest. Truffle veins peter out in 40 to 50 years; laying truffles down for the future seems to be a sensible precaution.

The season for the true *tartufi bianchi* is brief. It opens in September. During the second week of October, Alba is in full fete with banquets, speeches, visiting celebrities, and its very own truffle queen. By November the truffles are at their most potent and plentiful. By the end of January the ball is over.

In the Morra family's Hôtel Savona in Alba, visitors staying in rooms on the side are likely to be wakened early during the truffle season. The Morra canning and truffle-paste factory starts up at six in the morning. It is not so much the noise— a very moderate one as Italian noises go— that gets you out of bed, as the smell of truffles being bashed into a paste, emulsified with oil, and packed into tubes for a sandwich spread. "Truffle paste? Is there such a thing?" asks a *cavaliere* whose little shop window in the main street of Alba is pasted over with newspaper clippings and announcements to the effect that he is the *principe dei tartufi*. Certainly, somebody is due to succeed the Morra

dynasty, still regarded as the kings of the Alba truffle domain, even though the Morra manner of running a hotel and restaurant (its Michelin star must be the most misplaced in any of the whole Guide) is not so much regal as reminiscent of a Hollywood gangster farce. All the same, the Morra truffle paste not only exists but does retain something of the true scent and flavor which canned whole truffles rarely do.

Contradiction and confusion in all things concerning the white truffle are normal in Alba, where the most harmless questions are met with evasive answers, and where, for all the information one would ever be able to extract from the truffle dealers, the things might be brought by storks or found under gooseberry bushes.

In the market there is no display of the truffle merchants' wares. The knobbly brown nuggets are not weighed out and are not even to be seen unless you are a serious customer. Some three dozen silent men in somber suits stand in a huddle outside the perimeter of the poultry market. Only if you ask to see the truffles will one of these truffle men extract from his pocket a little paper- or cloth-wrapped parcel. You buy by nose and a sound, dry appearance.

About the storage of truffles the Albesi are comparatively communicative, if not very enlightening. "What is the best way to keep *tartufi*?"

"You wrap them in a piece of stuff..."

Another dealer interrupts, "No, you keep them in a jar of rice."

The *cavaliere* says this is nonsense. Rice, he says, makes the truffles wet, and they must have air. (Nobody here seems to have heard of wood shavings.) The *cavaliere* says jauntily that the ones we buy from him will last 10 days. They are packed in tissue paper in four-inch-square packing cases. They have so much air that on the drive back to Turin from Alba we are nearly strangled by the smell. It is glorious, but it is dissipating itself, and the truffles are weakening with every mile. By the time we get them back to London in three days they will be ghosts.

The *cavaliere*'s 10 days was a hefty overestimation, but his recommendation of the cooking at the Buoi Rossi (The Red Ox), the unmodernized Piedmontese country-town inn in the via Cavour, was worthwhile. In the quiet old courtyard, with its characteristic vista of Piedmontese arches and open loft stacked with the copper-red corncobs, we drank a bottle of red Dolcetto, a local wine and a dry and genuine one, and ate some bread and butter spread with the truffles. (This is one of the best ways of eating them if you can ever persuade a Piedmontese to allow you such a simple treat.) We returned three days running for meals.

The Red Ox is not mentioned in Michelin and is a simple *albergo-ristorante* where honest, decent, and cheap food, which includes a genuine *fonduta*, is to be had. There were also delicious pears baked in their skins and sprinkled with coarse sugar, and fresh, fat *fagioli alla regina*, oven-cooked. The local wines are all they should be. In typical Italian style the *padrona* was unable to tell us more about her first-class vintage Barolo than that it comes from her cousin, one Enrico Borgogno, a grower in Barolo itself, and that it was, she thought, 10 years old. The finer points of vintages and vintage years do not preoccupy Italian innkeepers. Unless it is standardized and commercialized out of all recognition, two bottles of precisely the same growth are likely to resemble each other in about the same degree as the black truffle of Périgord resembles the white one.

RICE,
BEANS
& LENTILS

Pilau rice

Measurements for pilau rice cooking are nearly always based on volume rather than weight. The use of a cup or glass for measuring the rice simplifies the recipes because the cooking liquid is measured in the same vessel, the success of the process depending largely upon the correct proportions of liquid to rice.

The cooking pot is also important, especially to those unfamiliar with the routine. Choose a saucepan or a two-handled casserole not too deep in proportion to its width. Whether of aluminum, iron, cast iron, copper, or earthernware is not important, provided the bottom is thick and even.

Those unfamiliar with rice cooking are advised to start by making a small quantity of pilau. The recipe once mastered, is easy to increase the quantities in proportion, and to experiment with different flavorings.

1 tumbler of Basmati rice, 2 tumblers of water.

Put the rice in a bowl and cover it with water. Let it soak for an hour or so.

Cooking and flavoring ingredients are 2 tablespoons of clarified butter (or ghee bought from an Indian provision store), 1 small onion, 4 cardamom pods, 2 teaspoons of cumin seeds, or ground cumin, a teaspoon of turmeric powder, 2 teaspoons of salt, a bay leaf or two, 2 tumblers of water.

Melt the butter in your rice-cooking pot or saucepan (for this quantity a 1.3–1.6-quart one is large enough) and in it cook the sliced onion for a few seconds, until it is translucent. It must not brown. This done, stir in the cardamom seeds extracted from their pods and the cumin seeds, both pounded in a mortar, and the turmeric. The latter is for coloring the rice a beautiful yellow, as well as for its flavor, and the object of cooking the spices in the fat is to develop their aromas before the rice is added. This is an important point.

Drain the rice, and put it into the butter and spice mixture. Stir it around until it glistens with the fat. Add the salt. Pour in the two tumblers of water and let it come to a boil fairly fast. Put in the bay leaf.

Let the rice cook steadily, uncovered, over medium heat until almost all the water is absorbed and holes begin to appear in the mass. This will take almost 10 minutes.

Now turn the heat as low as possible. Over the rice put a thickly folded absorbent dishcloth, and on top of the cloth (use an old one; the turmeric stains) the lid of the pan. Leave undisturbed, still over the lowest-possible heat, for 20 to 25 minutes. At the end of this time the rice should be quite tender and each grain will be separated. Fork it around and turn it into a warmed serving bowl.

The rice should be a fine yellow color and mildly spiced.

The pilau can be eaten as an accompaniment to spiced lamb or beef kebabs, but to my mind it is even nicer on its own, with the addition of a few golden raisins or raisins, soaked for an hour in water, heated up in a little saucepan, and mixed into the rice just before it is turned out of the saucepan for serving. Oven-toasted almonds or pine nuts make another attractive addition.

The tumbler I use for measuring holds scant 1 cup of basmati rice and ¾ cup of water.

Enough for two to three.

Saffron pilau rice

To make a dish of plain yellow rice which is to be a background for kebabs or some other dish, the rice is cooked as for the pilau on page 124. Instead of all the spices, use saffron to color the rice, and leave out the onions.

To prepare the saffron for coloring the rice proceed as follows: put as many whole saffron filaments as will cover a predecimal sixpenny piece (about ⅓ of a teaspoon) on a fireproof plate. Heat it for 5 to 10 minutes in a very moderate (300–325°F) oven. The saffron filaments can now be crumbled between the fingers and can then be stirred into the rice when it is in the saucepan and already glistening with the warmed clarified butter or fat.

The saffron does not immediately color the rice, even when the water is added. The yellow stain and the pungent aroma develop gradually. So do not panic and add a double dose until you have experience of the performance of this very pungent aromatic.

Enough for two to three.

Gratin of rice and zucchini

A delicate, rather mild dish.

1 pound of zucchini, 7 tablespoons of butter, 2 tablespoons of flour, generous 2 cups of milk, 3 tablespoons of Parmesan or Gruyère, 4 tablespoons of fine-quality rice, seasonings of salt, pepper, and nutmeg. A little extra butter for finishing the dish.

Prepare, grate, and cook the zucchini as described for the zucchini tian on p166, but using half the butter instead of olive oil. (This is a wonderful way of cooking zucchini to serve as a vegetable on its own—but you need a large pan.)

With the remaining butter, the flour, and warmed milk make a béchamel sauce. Season it well, not forgetting a little nutmeg. When it is well cooked and smooth, stir in the zucchini.

Cook the rice in boiling salted water, keeping it on the firm side. Have ready a lightly buttered gratin dish, approximately 8 x 2 inches, combine the zucchini-béchamel mixture with the rice, put it all into the dish, and smooth it down, lightly. On top sprinkle the Parmesan, and a little butter in tiny pieces.

Put the dish near the top of a moderate oven, 340°F and let it cook for 15 to 20 minutes, or 30 if the whole mixture has been heated up from cold. The top should be lightly golden and bubbly.

The first time I ever had this gratin of zucchini was at lunch in a village inn at Rians, near Aix-en-Provence. It was many years ago and I can still remember our meal. First came a typical Provençal hors d'oeuvre—pâté, tomato salad, olives, a few slices of salami—then the zucchini dish, quite on its own, followed by a daube of beef served sizzling-hot in a casserole brought to the table and left on it so that we could help ourselves. Then, as an alternative to the fruit, or ice cream, one would expect at the end of such a meal we were offered little bowls of a most delicious jam, homemade from green melons. There was, by the way, no vegetable of any kind with the beef stew. We had good bread with which to mop up the juices, and that was enough.

Enough for four.

Tomatoes with rice and walnut stuffing

For 8–10 large tomatoes, the ingredients for the stuffing are ½ cup of rice, a chopped shallot, scant ½ cup shelled and chopped walnuts, a dessertspoon of currants, the grated peel of half a lemon, 2 tablespoons of butter, pepper, salt, nutmeg, and 1 egg, a little olive oil or extra melted butter.

Boil the rice, keeping it slightly underdone. Drain and while still warm mix it with all the other ingredients. Slice off the tops of the tomatoes, scoop out the pulp, add it to the rice mixture, fill the tomatoes, piling the stuffing up into a mound. Replace the tops, put them in an oiled baking pan or dish, pour a few drops of oil or melted butter over each, and bake in the oven at 340°F; about half an hour should be sufficient.

Enough for four to five.

Giulia's tomato sauce and dry rice

Giulia Piccini was Tuscan; she came from a hill village near Florence. Giulia's cooking was, like herself, elegant and delicate.

With a dish of dry rice, cooked in the manner of a pilau, Giulia used to serve the simplest-possible tomato sauce. She sliced ripe tomatoes into a bowl, mixed them with olive oil, wine vinegar, salt, pepper, and a scrap of onion. The important points are to prepare the mixture two hours in advance, and immediately before serving to stir in a pinch of sugar.

For the *riso secco* use long-grain rice. Chop half a small onion and put it in a deep saucepan or casserole with olive oil and butter. When the onion turns pale gold, extract it, stir in 2½ cups rice, and let it cook until it turns a pale-blond color; now pour in salted water or broth and cook, covered, for 20 minutes. Take care that the rice is not too liquid; it is sufficient for the water to cover it by one finger's depth or less; when cooked, turn it onto a serving dish, and on top put, here and there, some flakes of butter and some grated cheese.

The tomato sauce is served separately. *Riso secco* may sound dull, but the contrast of the hard, hot rice and the cold tomato "salad" is absolutely delectable. It's important to remember that the rice should not be shaken about or disturbed.

Enough for six.

Bruscandoli

One fine morning early in May, 1969, with my sister Diana Grey and her husband, I arrived at the island of Torcello to lunch at Cipriani's lovely little Locanda, famous both for its cooking and its charm. I knew the place of old; so did the fourth member of our party. To my sister and brother-in-law it was new. This was their first visit to Venice. For all of us the trip was a particularly magical one.

When we had settled at our table and ordered our food—the pitchers of house wine were at our elbows as we sat down—I became aware of a couple at a neighboring table exclaiming with rapture over their food. They were a handsome and elegant pair. I wondered what was so special about the rice dish which was giving them such pleasure. They in turn noticed my curiosity. With beautiful Italian manners they passed some across to me, explaining that it was a risotto unique to Venice and unique to this particular season. It was made with a green vegetable called *bruscandoli*, or *brucelando*. Wild asparagus, so they explained. It was so good that I called the waiter and changed my order. A most delicate and remarkable risotto it was. The manager of the restaurant told me that only during the first 10 days of May can this particular wild asparagus be found in the Venetian countryside.

Next day, we all went to another of the lagoon islands, to lunch at Romano's on Burano. Surprise. There were our friends again, and again the green risotto was on the menu. They had of course ordered it. So did we. This time they told me I might find some *brucelando* in the Rialto market if I went early enough in the morning. Hurry though; the season ends any day now. When the charming and splendid pair had left, I asked the proprietor of the tavern who they were. Ah, you mean the Isotta-Fraschini? The inheritors of the name of that wonderful and glamorous automobile of the Twenties and Thirties, no less. No wonder they carried about them the aura of romance, and, he especially, of the authentic Italian *magnifico*. So, to me, the name of Isotta-Fraschini is now indissolubly linked with the memory of those extraordinary and subtle risotti of the Venetian lagoons.

We went again to Torcello to eat *bruscandoli*, I went to the Rialto market, found an old woman selling a few bunches of it—it's the last of the year, she said— took it back to my hotel, and stuck it in a glass so that I could make a drawing of it. When I came back in the evening, the zealous chambermaid had thrown it away. No, next morning there was no old lady selling *bruscandoli* in the market. For once it was true, that warning: "Tomorrow it will be finished."

I searched the cookbooks and the dictionaries for more details of the wild asparagus. I could find no descriptions, no references. Months later, in a little book about Venetian specialties I discovered the following sentence: "*Le minestre più usate sono quelle di riso: con bruscandoli (luppolo) kumo (finocchio selvatico)…*" So *bruscandoli* is Venetian for *luppoli*. And *luppoli* or *cime di luppolo* are wild hop-shoots.

It is of course well known that hop-shoots have a flavor much akin to that of asparagus, and the confusion is a common one. All the same, it was curious that neither the local Venetians to whom I talked, nor the knowledgeable Isotta-Fraschini couple should have known that hop-shoots rather than asparagus were used in those famous risotti. Maybe they did but didn't know the alternative word (in the Milan region they have yet another name, *loertis*) and thought that wild asparagus was a near enough approximation. The truth is, that when I bought the *brucelando* in the market, it didn't look much like any kind of asparagus, so I was suspicious. But it didn't look like hops, either. And wild hop-shoots I had never before seen.

Research has yielded various other regional Italian dishes made with *bruscandoli* or *luppoli*. In her little book *La Cucina Romana* dealing with the old specialties of Roman cooking, Ada Boni gives a recipe for a *zuppa di luppoli*, and I have heard of a *frittata* or flat omelet with hop-shoots from Tuscany and also in the more northerly region of Brianza. In Belgium hop-shoots are equally a specialty. They are called *jets de houblon*.

The cooking and serving of risotto

To achieve a true risotto, the very first requisite is the right type of rice. Italian rice is quite unlike any other. The grains are large, round, and pearly, with a clearly defined hard white heart which prevents the rice, turning mushy and is responsible for the characteristic flavor and for the unique consistency of a risotto. The three Italian rices to use are arborio, carnaroli, and vialone nano.

In Italy risotto is invariably eaten as a first course and in restaurants it is listed on the menu with the soups. Indeed, a risotto almost is a soup. Almost—but just not quite.

If you have never eaten a risotto correctly cooked in Venice or in Milan it is difficult to appreciate that there is a split-second in the cooking of the rice—just as for scrambled eggs —when the consistency is exactly right. It is neither too liquid nor too compact. It is light, every grain is separate although bound together in a homogenous whole by the starch which has amalgamated with the cooking liquid. Suddenly, dismayingly, all is lost. Your risotto has become heavy, stodgy. It is still perfectly edible and probably tastes very good. It is just that its elegance and distinction have vanished.

Shellfish and fresh green vegetables are the two staple flavorings of the Venetian risotto. Both are used in astonishingly small quantity in proportion to the rice. Both make dishes of great finesse.

While it is vain to hope to reproduce an Adriatic shellfish dish unless the Adriatic coast is where you live, it does seem feasible to attempt a vegetable risotto cooked along the lines of the Venetian one, even though the vegetables will be different and the end-product possibly unfamiliar to a Venetian.

Vegetable risotto

10 dried mushrooms, approx. 5 lettuce leaves, 1 leaf of a fennel bulb, 1 small onion, ⅓ cup of butter, ¾–scant 1 cup of Piedmontese arborio rice, 2½–3 cups of water, 2 tablespoons of grated Parmesan, salt, nutmeg.

Use a 1.3-quart heavy saucepan. Soak the mushrooms in warm water for half an hour. Drain and cut very small. Shred the lettuce leaves and finely dice the fennel. Peel and chop the onion.

Melt 3 tablespoons butter in the pan and cook the lettuce and fennel until soft. Lift out the vegetables, leaving behind the butter. Put in a little more butter if necessary and cook the onion for 1 minute until translucent. Add the rice, and stir it around until it glistens with butter. Pour in scant 2 cups of boiling water and cook, uncovered, over medium heat until all the liquid is absorbed. It will take about 15 minutes.

When it begins to look dry, stir in the mushrooms, 1 teaspoon of salt, and another ⅔ cup of boiling water. At this stage it needs watching. With a wooden fork, which doesn't break the grains, stir the rice and taste to see how tender it is. The grains must retain a slight resistance and the risotto must be liquid.

Stir in the lettuce and fennel with the Parmesan cheese, a generous grating of nutmeg, and the remaining butter.

Enough for two.

Green vegetable risotto

3 small zucchini, 7 tablespoons of butter, 1 bunch of watercress, 2 shallots, 1½–1¾ cups of arborio rice, 5 cups of water, 3 tablespoons of grated Parmesan, nutmeg, salt.

Use a 2.1-quart heavy pan.

Peel the zucchini in alternate strips, slice lengthwise into four pieces, then cut into tiny dice. Cook them in 2 tablespoons butter in a small pan until just soft. Clean the watercress, discard all cottony and ragged parts of the stalks, cook the remainder in 1 tablespoon butter for 1 minute, then chop. Melt another 3 tablespoons butter in the heavy pan and cook the chopped shallots for 1 minute. Stir in the rice and add 2½ cups of boiling water. Cook as described on p135, adding more water as necessary until the rice is cooked to the right consistency.

The zucchini and watercress go in at the end; to reheat the watercress before adding to the risotto, put it into the pan with the zucchini. Finish the risotto with the Parmesan, remaining butter, and a grating of nutmeg.

Enough for four.

Risotto with mushrooms

This is a very simple form of risotto.

Take 1½ cups of Italian rice, 5 cups of vegetable or chicken stock, 1 wineglass of oil, 1 medium onion chopped fine, 2 cloves of garlic chopped, ¼ pound of white mushrooms cut into slices. Into a heavy sauté pan put the oil and as soon as it is warm put in the onion, the garlic, and the mushrooms. As soon as the onion begins to brown, add the rice and stir until it takes on a transparent look. This is the moment to start adding the stock, which should be kept just on a boil by the side of the fire. Pour in about 2 cups at a time, and go on stirring and adding stock each time it has been absorbed. The whole process is done over low flame, and in about 45 to 50 minutes, the risotto should be ready. It should be creamy, homogeneous, but on no account reduced to oatmeal. One must be able to taste each grain of rice although it is not separated as in pilau. Grated Parmesan cheese is served with it, and sometimes stirred in before bringing the risotto to the table. In any case a risotto must be eaten immediately it is ready, and cannot be kept warm in the oven, steamed over a pan of boiling water, or otherwise kept waiting.

Enough for four.

Fool

Egyptian brown beans

Fool (brown beans) are the staple food of the Egyptian peasant. 1 pound of these beans and 6 tablespoons of red lentils are washed and put into an earthen or copper casserole with 3 cups of water. This is brought to a boil and then left for hours and hours—all night usually—on a low charcoal fire. If necessary more water can be added. Salt is not put in until the cooking is finished, and olive oil is poured over them in the plate, and sometimes hard-boiled eggs are served with them. The lid of the casserole should be removed as little as possible, or the beans will go black.

The way I cook Egyptian dried brown beans (to be bought in Middle Eastern stores) on a modern cooker is as follows: soak scant 1½ cups of them in cold water for about 12 hours. Put them into an earthenware pot well covered with fresh water (about 2–2½ cups). Put the covered pot in the lowest-possible oven and leave undisturbed all day or all night, or for a minimum of 7 hours. When they are quite soft and most of the water is absorbed, decant them into a shallow serving bowl or dish, season with salt, moisten with plenty of fruity olive oil and lemon juice—or, better still, the juice of fresh limes. Serve separately a plate of hard-boiled eggs. This is a very filling, nourishing, and cheap dish. Cans of ready-cooked Egyptian brown beans are also available; they are time-saving but still require a good hour of extra cooking, and of course the ritual seasoning of olive oil and lemon.

Enough for three or four.

Haricots à la bretonne

Dried haricot beans with onions and tomatoes

This way of cooking beans makes a dish which is a good background for eggs as well as a useful vegetable to serve with all kinds of meat and sausages.

Scant 1½ cups of medium-size dried white beans, previously soaked overnight, are cooked in water to cover by about 2 inches, with the addition of an onion stuck with a clove, a carrot, a small piece of celery, a bouquet of thyme, parsley, and bay leaf. Add salt only at the end. When they are tender, drain them, setting aside the liquid. Chop the onion which has cooked with them and fry it in butter; add 2 peeled and chopped tomatoes, fry 2 minutes, dilute with a little of the reserved liquid. Add to the beans; reheat them gently, adding, if available, a little juice from a roast, or meat glaze.

Enough for three to four.

Lenticche en umido

Stewed lentils

Scant 2 cups brown lentils, olive oil, a small onion, mint, garlic.

Wash the lentils and pick out any pieces of grit. There is no need to soak them. Cover the bottom of a thick pan with olive oil, and when it is warm melt the sliced onion in it. Add the lentils, and as soon as they have absorbed the oil pour 5 cups of hot water over them. Add a clove of garlic and a sprig of fresh mint. Cover the pan and stew steadily for 20 to 25 minutes. By that time the lentils should be soft and the liquid nearly all absorbed. Now season with salt and pepper. Also good cold, with the addition of fresh olive oil and hard-boiled eggs.

Enough for four or five.

Chickpeas or haricot beans with a Turkish dressing

Cook scant 1½ cups chickpeas as described in Tuoni e lampo, p107, or beans as in Haricots à la bretonne, p143.

Scant 1 cup of shelled walnuts, a clove of garlic. 4 tablespoons of dried bread crumbs, a breakfast cup of vegetable or chicken stock, or milk, salt, lemon juice, cayenne pepper, parsley, or mint.

Pound the walnuts and garlic to a paste; stir in the bread crumbs, then the stock or milk, season with salt, lemon juice, and cayenne pepper. The sauce should be about the consistency of cream. Stir the dressing into the chickpeas or beans and sprinkle the dish with fresh herbs before serving.

Enough for three to four.

Fasoulia

The Greek name for haricot beans. People who appreciate the taste of genuine olive oil in their food will like this dish. Soak scant 1½ cups of beans for 12 hours. Heat half a tumbler of olive oil in a deep pan; put in the strained beans; lower the heat; stir the beans and let them simmer gently for 10 minutes, adding 2 cloves of garlic, a bay leaf, a branch of thyme, and a dessertspoon of tomato paste. Add boiling water to cover the beans by about 1 inch. Cook them over moderate fire for 3 hours. The liquid should have reduced sufficiently to form a thickish sauce. Squeeze in the juice of a lemon, add some raw onions cut into rings, some salt and black pepper, and let them cool.

Enough for three to four.

MAIN DISHES

Pumpkin and tomato gratin

A 2 pound piece of pumpkin, 1 pound of tomatoes, 2 stalks of celery or the tops of a whole small head, 3 tablespoons of butter, salt, garlic if you like, parsley, about 4 tablespoons of coarse bread crumbs.

Peel the pumpkin, discard the seeds and the cottony center core; cut into small chunks. Skin and chop the tomatoes. Wash and chop the celery.

In a large heavy skillet heat 2 tablespoons of the butter, put in the celery, the pumpkin, and 1 scant tablespoon of salt. Cook gently, uncovered, until the pumpkin is soft and just beginning to look slightly jammy. Transfer it to a shallow gratin dish. In the same pan cook the tomatoes, with the garlic if you are using it, a little more salt and some chopped parsley. When most of the moisture has evaporated and the tomatoes are almost in a puree, mix with the pumpkin, smooth down the top (the dish should be quite full), cover with the bread crumbs and the remaining butter cut into tiny pieces, stand the dish on a baking sheet, and cook near the top of a fairly hot oven, 350°F, for 35 to 40 minutes, until the top surface is golden and crisp.

Enough for four.

Ratatouille

Ratatouille is a Provençale ragout of vegetables, usually peppers, onions, tomatoes, and eggplants, stewed very slowly in oil. This dish has the authentic aromatic flavor of Provençale food.

3 or 4 tomatoes, 2 eggplants, 2 large onions, 2 red or green bell peppers, oil, salt, and pepper.

Peel and chop the tomatoes and cut the unpeeled eggplants into squares. Slice the onions and peppers. Put the onions into a skillet or sauté pan with plenty of oil, not too hot. When they are getting soft add first the peppers and eggplants, and, 10 minutes later, the tomatoes. Season. The vegetables should not be fried, but stewed in the oil, so simmer in a covered pan for the first 30 minutes, uncovered for the last 10. By this time they should have absorbed most of the oil.

Enough for four.

Peperonata
Sweet pepper and tomato stew

A large onion, olive oil, butter, 8 red bell peppers, salt, 10 good ripe tomatoes.

Brown the sliced onion very lightly in a mixture of olive oil and butter. Add the peppers, cleaned, the seeds removed, and cut into strips; season them with salt. Simmer them for about 15 minutes, with the cover on the pan. Now add the tomatoes, peeled and quartered, and cook for another 30 minutes. There should not be too much oil, as the tomatoes provide enough liquid to cook the peppers, and the resulting mixture should be fairly dry. Garlic can be added if you like.

To store for a few days in the refrigerator, pack the peperonata in a jar, and float enough oil on the top to seal the contents. Enough for six or seven people, but peperonata is so good when reheated that it is worth making a large amount at one time.

The Great English Aphrodisiac

It was a subject awaiting an author. The potato, its history as a member of the botanical family *Solanaceae*, its adoption by man as a cultivated plant, and the record of its spread throughout the world, found a very remarkable author. He was a young doctor, whose active career in medicine had been cut short by illness while still in his twenties. By the time he was 32, living a life of ease in a beautiful Hertfordshire village, happily married, free from financial worries, Redcliffe Salaman found himself completely restored to health and able once more to lead a physically active life. His winters were sufficiently taken up with fox-hunting but, lacking enthusiasm for golf, tennis, and cricket, he found his summers empty of interesting occupation. After a false start in the field of Mendelian research and the study of the heredity of butterflies, hairless mice, guinea pigs, and the like, this singular young man turned to his gardener for advice as to a suitable subject for research. Something ordinary, such as a common kitchen garden vegetable, Dr Salaman stipulated.

The gardener, whose name was Evan Jones, was that archetype, the omniscient one known ever since Adam vacated Eden. Jones had no hesitation in advising Dr Salaman that if he wanted to spend his spare time in the study of vegetables, then he had better choose the potato. Because, said Jones, "I know more about the potato than any man living." It was then 1906. Forty-three years later, in 1949, Redcliffe Salaman's extraordinary study, *The History and Social Influence of the Potato*, was published by the Cambridge University Press.

"A work of profound and accurate scholarship," commented the scientific journal *Nature*. "A great, in many respects a noble work" was *The Spectator*'s verdict. Reprinted in 1970 , and again last November, with a new introduction and corrections by J. G Hawkes, the book remains a major work of reference on its subject.

With the exception of recipes, no aspect of the potato story was neglected by Salaman. He traces its origins in the Andes, and its deep significance in the lives of the Incas, to its arrival and reception in Europe in the second half of the sixteenth century, its fatal planting and all-too-rapid spread in Ireland, its entirely mythical connection with Virginia, the long unresolved confusion of identity between the tubers of the sweet potato, *Ipomoea batatas*, and those of the totally unrelated common potato, *Solanum tuberosum*, further complicated by the late arrival in Europe of a red herring in the shape of *Helianthus tuberosus*, known to us as the Jerusalem artichoke, to the French as *topinambour*, and to the Germans as *Erdbirn* or earth pear. In France arose an even odder confusion created apparently by the French horticulturalist Olivier de Serre who, in 1600, published his *Théâtre d'Agriculture* in which he offered a description of the potato plant comparing its tubers to truffles, saying that it was often called by the same name, *cartouffles*. As to the taste, said de Serres, "The cook so dresses all of them that one can recognize but little difference between them."

Olivier de Serres was not alone in likening potatoes to truffles. To the Italians at the same period, common potato tubers were *tartuffoli* or *taratouffli*, and under the latter name two were sent by a correspondent to the famous Belgian-born botanist Charles de L'Ecluse in Vienna, where in 1588 he was employed working on the Emperor Maximilian's gardens. A few years later, in 1595, L'Ecluse, or Clusius as he called himself in Latin, accepted a professorship in Leyden University, and from then until his death in 1609 one of his many preoccupations was the encouragement of potato cultivation—of the common potato, that is—throughout Europe.

At the same time—although Salaman does not specifically point this out—to most Italian contemporaries of Olivier de Serres and Charles de L'Ecluse, potatoes undoubtedly meant *patatas* or sweet potatoes, and not the common potato. In Spain, particularly around Seville and Malaga, *patatas* had been established early in the sixteenth century. It was probably from Spain, therefore, that they reached Italy. In both countries they were appreciated for their sweetness and the resemblance of their flesh to that of sweet chestnuts, which at the time were commonly served with the dessert fruits. Roasted in the ashes, peeled, sugared, sliced into white wine, or into a sugar syrup, potatoes were also candied, as in those days was almost every fruit, vegetable, and flower in sight, from primroses to pumpkins, lettuce stalks to wild cherries. In 1557, a Spanish writer, G. F Oviedo y Valdes, giving an account of Hispaniola (Haiti), compared *patatas* favorably to marzipan. A higher recommendation you could not give.

In England, too, potatoes imported from Spain were quickly accepted as a delicacy. They wouldn't, of course, grow in the English climate, and the price was high. Salaman cites an instance of two pounds of potatoes "for the queen's table" costing, in 1599, 2s 6d per pound. Regardless of price, or perhaps because of it, they took the fancy of the luxury-loving Tudor gentry.

Recipes for candying potatoes were tried out and written down in household receipt books, and before long the tubers were appearing as an ingredient in expensive pie fillings. A receipt for one such found its way into print in a little book promisingly titled *The Good Huswife's Jewell* published as early as 1596. Thomas Dawson, who claimed authorship of the book, gave the ingredients as two quinces, two or three burre roots (pears, says Salaman. But why roots?), an ounce of dates, and just one "potaton," cooked in wine, strained, mixed with rose water, sugar, spices, butter, the brains of three or four cock-sparrows, and eight egg yolks, all to be cooked until thick enough to be consigned to the pastry shell. If the sparrows' brains and the potaton didn't give the game away, the title of the receipt was clear enough. "To make a tarte that is a courage to a man or woman" simply meant that the brew was an aphrodisiac—although just why sparrows' brains were so associated I have never discovered. How the Spanish potato came to join the list of prized English aphrodisiacs is explained by Salaman in a diverting chapter, one which he himself had clearly had a good deal of fun researching.

In the works of late Elizabethan and Jacobean dramatists, including Shakespeare, Salaman found quite a storehouse of bawdry concerning the perfectly innocent Spanish tubers. They were of course luxuries. As such they came to have the same saucy connotations as Champagne, caviar, oysters, and truffles to later generations. In 1617 potatoes were including among the foods dubbed "whetstones of venery" by George Chapman. In the same year, John Fletcher had soldiers disguised as pedlars singing licentious songs and making impudent fun of an elderly gentleman: "Will your Lordship please to taste a fine potato? T'will advance your withered state. Fill your Honor full of noble itches."

In only slightly less crude terms Fletcher, again, suggests the potato as a revivifier of a woman's lost vigor; "Will your Ladyship have a potato pie? 'Tis a good stirring dish for an old lady after a long Lent." Not that everyone thought it necessary to abstain from this overstimulating food during Lent. In 1634 the prolific early Stuart letter-writer, James Howell, castigated people who while abstaining from "Flesh, Fowl and Fish" on Ash Wednesday, made up for the penance by eating luxurious "Potatoes in a dish Done O'er with Amber, or a mess of Ringos in a Spanish dress." Ringos were eryngoes, roots of the sea-holly, usually candied, and had long preceded the potato as a reputed aphrodisiac.

The absurdist aspect of the aphrodisiac story was that when eventually the common potato, *Solanum tuberosum*, superceded *Ipomoea batatas* in English esteem, the reputation of the exotic Spanish potato was for a time transferred to our own homegrown tuber. In continental Europe, the eggplant and the tomato, both members of the same *Solanaceae* family, were in their turn attributed with the possession of aphrodisiac powers.

Galette de pommes de terre

Peel about 1½ pounds of potatoes and slice them very thinly and evenly. Wash them in plenty of cold water. In a thick skillet heat a tablespoon of butter and one of oil (the mixture of butter and oil gives a good flavor, and the oil prevents the butter from burning).

Put the potatoes into the pan and spread them evenly; season with nutmeg, salt, and ground black pepper; turn the heat down as soon as they start to cook, cover the pan, and leave them cooking gently for 15 minutes; by this time the undersurface will be browned and the potatoes coagulated in such a way as to form a pancake; turn the galette over and leave the other side to brown for 3 or 4 minutes; serve either turned out whole onto a flat dish or cut into quarters.

Enough for four.

La truffado

This is a peasant dish from the Auvergne, made with fromage de Cantal, which is something like English Cheshire cheese, which can be used instead,

Slice 1 pound of raw potatoes thinly and cook them in a skillet as for the Galette de pommes de terre (above), with the addition of a clove of garlic finely chopped. When the potatoes are almost cooked, add the cheese, about 2 ounces cut in very small pieces, and turn the potatoes once or twice, so that the cheese spreads all over them.

Cover the pan, turn the heat off, and let the cheese melt in the heat of the pan for 5 minutes before serving.

Enough for two or three.

NOTE: Cantal can now often be found in good cheese stores and delicatessens in the US.

Gratin dauphinois

Gratin dauphinois is a rich and filling regional dish from the Dauphiné. Some recipes, Escoffier's and Austin de Croze's among them, include cheese and eggs, making it very similar to a gratin Savoyard: but other regional authorities declare that the authentic gratin dauphinois is made only with potatoes and thick fresh cream. I give the second version, which is, I think, the better one; it is also the easier. And if it seems to the thrifty-minded outrageously extravagant to use one-and-a-quarter cups of cream to one pound of potatoes, I can only say that to me it seems a more satisfactory way of enjoying cream than pouring it over canned peaches or chocolate mousse.

Peel 1 pound of yellow potatoes, and slice them in even circles no thicker than a cent; this operation is very easy with the aid of the mandolin. Rinse them thoroughly in cold water —this is most important—then shake them dry in a cloth. Put them in layers in a shallow earthenware dish which has been rubbed with garlic and well buttered. Season with pepper and salt. Pour 1¼ cups of thick cream over them; strew with little pieces of butter; cook them for 1½ hours in a low oven at 300°F. During the last 10 minutes turn the oven up fairly high to get a fine golden crust on the potatoes. Serve in the dish in which they have cooked; it is not easy to say how many people this will serve; two, or three, or four, according to their capacity, and what there is to follow.

Much depends also upon the quality of the potatoes used. Firm waxy varieties such as the kipfler and the pink fir-apple (or red potatoes), which appear occasionally on the London market, make a gratin lighter and also more authentic than that made with routine commercial King Edward or Majestics, which are in every respect second-best.

The best way, in my view, of appreciating the charm of a gratin dauphinois is to present the dish entirely on its own, as a first course to precede broiled or plain roast meat or poultry, or a cold joint to be eaten with a simple green salad.

Sweet-sour cabbage

For this you need a large, wide sauté pan, or a Chinese wok. The recipe, however, is an Italian one.

Ingredients are: a good hard little white cabbage weighing about 2 pounds, or half a larger one, olive oil, salt, sugar, wine vinegar, parsley.

Cut out and discard the hard stalk part from the cabbage. Slice the rest into thin ribbons. Heat 2 or 3 tablespoons of olive oil in the pan. Throw in the cabbage before the oil gets too hot. Sauté it quickly, turning it over and over with a wooden spatula. Add salt—say, 2 teaspoons—but you have to taste. Cover the pan. Leave it for 5 minutes. Uncover it, stir, and turn again, adding 2 level tablespoons of sugar and 2 of wine vinegar. Cover and leave for another 5 minutes. Taste for the seasoning. Turn into a shallow serving dish or salad bowl. Strew with chopped parsley.

This is good as a vegetable dish on its own. Or serve it as a salad with ham or cold roast pork.

Enough for four.

Sweet-sour cabbage with spiced prunes

Cook the cabbage as in the recipe above. During the final minutes of cooking add 8 or 10 spiced prunes prepared as in the recipe on p187. A beautiful dish. But take great care that the cabbage is still a little bit crisp and that the prunes retain their identity.

Enough for four.

Blettes à la crème
Chard in cream sauce

This is a very everyday dish in the southern Rhône country. Just how good it is depends mainly upon how much care one takes over the cream sauce. For 1 pound of *blettes* or *poirée*, the chard which one sees displayed for sale in huge bundles in every market in the southern Rhône country, make a cream sauce with 3 tablespoons of butter, 2 tablespoons of flour, scant 2 cups of milk, seasonings of salt, pepper, and nutmeg, and about ⅓ cup of heavy cream.

Melt the butter; then, off the stove, stir in the flour. When it is smooth add the warmed milk, little by little. When the mixture looks creamy, return the saucepan to very low heat, add the rest of the milk. Season lightly with salt, freshly milled pepper, and a scrap of nutmeg. Let the sauce almost imperceptibly bubble for 15 to 20 minutes, stirring frequently.

Now add the cream. The sauce should be very smooth, ivory-colored, and no thicker than cream. You can now if you like add a tablespoon or two of finely grated Gruyère or Parmesan cheese, just as a seasoning. And if your sauce has turned lumpy, press it through a strainer.

Clean the chard, discard the hard leaf stalks and central veins, cook it in just a very little water, salt it lightly halfway through the cooking. Drain it in a colander, press out excess moisture by putting a plate and weight on top. Chop it roughly.

In a gratin dish pour a little of your cream sauce. On top put the chard and cover with the rest of the sauce. The gratin dish should be quite full. Spread a few tiny pieces of butter over the surface, heat in a moderate oven, 350°F, for about 20 minutes, until the sauce is just faintly golden and bubbling.

Of course, all this is a trouble to do, but it makes an excellent and not very expensive first dish . It is one I often serve before a simple meat dish, beef, lamb, or veal, which is probably already cooking in the oven before the vegetable dish goes in.

Enough for four.

Sformato di piselli freschi
Sformato of green peas

A *sformato*, a dish which features largely in Italian home cooking but never in restaurants, is a cross between a soufflé and what we should call a dessert. It is a capital way of using green peas, green beans, spinach, fennel, or any vegetables which are plentiful but no longer in the tender stage when they may be eaten simply with butter. A *sformato* is a trouble to prepare, but requires fewer eggs than a soufflé and is not at all exacting to cook. It may be served as a separate course with some kind of sauce, or as a background to meat (*scaloppini*, for example), or lamb chops, or small pieces of veal broiled on a skewer.

For a sformato of fresh green peas you need about 3 pounds of peas, a small onion, ⅓ cup of butter, generous ¼ cup of grated Parmesan, a tablespoon of flour, a cup of milk, 1½–2 ounces of cooked ham (optional), 3 eggs.

First sauté the chopped onion lightly in 2 tablespoons butter; add the shelled peas and cover them with water. Season them with salt and let them simmer until they are completely cooked.

While the peas are cooking, prepare a little very thick béchamel with 2 tablespoons of butter, a tablespoon of flour, and the cup of milk previously heated. Season it well, add to it the grated cheese, and the ham cut into small strips, if you are using it. When the peas are cooked, strain them and put them through a strainer (or whiz in a food processor), keeping a few apart. Return the puree to the saucepan with a nut of butter, and add the béchamel and the whole peas. Give it a stir or two so that the mixture is well amalgamated. Let it cool, and then stir in the yolks of eggs, and lastly the beaten whites. Pour the whole mixture into a buttered cake pan or soufflé dish, stand it in a bain marie, and steam it, with a cover on the pan, for about an hour. Turn the *sformato* out onto a dish (which can be tricky to do), or serve it in its own dish, and either pour a sauce over it or arrange around it whatever meat it is to accompany. (Apart from meat, shrimp, or scallops cooked in butter go nicely with the green pea *sformato*, or a mushroom sauce (see p98), or poached eggs.)

Enough for four. The *sformato* may be made very successfully with frozen green peas.

Parmigiana
Eggplant pie

2 pounds of eggplants, salt, pepper, flour, olive oil, ½ pound of mozzarella cheese, 2 ounces of Parmesan, ⅔ cup of freshly made tomato sauce (p98).

Peel the eggplants and cut them into long, thin slices. Salt them and put them into a colander to drain for an hour or two. Dust them with flour, fry them gently in olive oil, and drain them on paper towels. Put a little oil in the bottom of a china soufflé dish or a deep cake pan. Put in a layer of the eggplants, cover with thin slices of mozzarella, and then the tomato sauce. Continue in this way until the eggplants are all used up. Cover with the grated Parmesan and sprinkle oil over the top. Cook in a moderate (350°F) oven for 20 to 30 minutes.

Enough for four to five.

Piments doux farcis au riz
Sweet peppers stuffed with rice

Stuffed sweet peppers, whether in France, Italy, England, or anywhere else, very often become a very heavy and stodgy dish. The common mistake is to cram the peppers too full with too solid and rich a mixture. This recipe, said to be of Corsican origin, makes a good dish to serve as a hot first course, and shows how small a quantity of stuffing is necessary for peppers.

Ingredients are 1 teacup of rice, 2 to 3 tablespoons of finely chopped parsley mixed with a little marjoram or wild thyme, lemon juice, olive oil, 4 large red or green sweet bell peppers, salt, and freshly milled pepper.

Boil the rice, keeping it a little undercooked. Drain and season it; stir in the parsley mixture, some lemon juice, and a little olive oil. Cut the peppers in half lengthwise. Remove all the core and the seeds and rinse the peppers under running cold water to make sure that no single seed is left. Put 2 tablespoons of the rice mixture into each half-pepper; pour a film of olive oil into a shallow baking dish, put in the stuffed peppers, cover them, and cook in a gentle oven, 325°F, for about an hour. From time to time baste the peppers with the oil in the dish, adding more if necessary. The rice should remain moist, and no hard crust should form on the top.

The dish is usually served hot but is also good cold as an hors-d'oeuvre. There should be ample for four.

Tian of zucchini

8–12 ounces potatoes boiled in their skins, approximately 4 tablespoons of olive oil, a small clove of garlic, seasonings of salt, nutmeg, and freshly milled black pepper, 8 ounces of zucchini, 5 or 6 eggs, 2 heaping tablespoons each of parsley and grated cheese, a few spinach or sorrel leaves if you happen to have them.

For these quantities you need a dish of 8 inches diameter and 2 inches deep.

First, peel the cooked potatoes. Cut them into cubes, put them into the earthenware dish with 2 tablespoons of olive oil, the chopped garlic, and seasoning of salt and pepper. Let them warm in the uncovered dish in a low oven, 300°F, while you prepare and cook the zucchini. The best way to do this is simply to wash them, trim off the ends, and leave them unpeeled except for any blemished parts. Instead of slicing them, grate them coarsely on a stainless-steel grater. Put them straight into a sauté pan or wide skillet with a couple of tablespoons of olive oil (or butter if you prefer), sprinkle them with salt, and cook them gently for 5 minutes, with a cover on the pan.

Now break the eggs into a large bowl. Beat them until frothy. Add the chopped parsley and any other fresh greenery you may have—this could include watercress and lettuce as well as spinach or sorrel, uncooked, and simply cut up with scissors— the cheese, salt, pepper, nutmeg, then the warm zucchini. Last of all, but gently to avoid breaking them, stir in the potatoes. Tip the whole mixture into the dish, sprinkle the top with a little oil, and return it, uncovered, to the oven, now heated to 375°F.

Leave the tian to bake for 25 to 30 minutes until it is well and evenly risen. The top should be a fine and appetizing golden-brown. For serving hot, leave it in the dish, and simply cut it into wedges, like a cake. If you intend to serve it cold, let it cool before turning it out onto a serving plate. If it is for a picnic leave it in the cooking dish, put a plate on top, and envelop it in a cloth knotted at the top.

A tian made with the quantities given should be enough for four to six people.

Tarte aux asperges
Asparagus tart

For the pie dough: generous 1¾ cups plain flour, a pinch of salt, ¾ cup butter. For the filling: 2 pounds asparagus, sugar, scant 2 cups béchamel sauce made with milk or cream, ½ cup grated cheese.

Knead the flour, salt, and butter together, adding a little water to make a paste. Prepare this 1 hour before cooking, if possible.

Prepare the asparagus very carefully, peeling off the dry outer skin of the stalks. Put them tied in a bunch and heads uppermost into boiling salted water, to which you add also a teaspoon of sugar and cook them for 10 minutes (a little longer if they are very large ones). Drain them and cut each asparagus into 3 or 4 pieces, discarding the hard part at the ends.

Roll out your pie dough, line a flat buttered pie pan (9–10 inches) with it, cover the inside and the edges with paper towels, and put the usual beans into the paper to keep the dough flat. Bake it in a hot oven (400°F) for 20 minutes. Heat up the béchamel gently while the pie dough is baking. Now add the grated cheese to the prepared béchamel and, off the fire, the asparagus.

Take the paper and the beans off the pie dough, fill with the asparagus mixture, put it into the oven to brown, and serve hot.

Enough for four to five.

Tarte à l'oignon
Onion tart

In nearly every French province there are recipes for onion tarts, sometimes made with a puree, sometimes with fried onions, green scallions, or leeks. Some people add bacon, some cream. In Provence the equivalent is the Pissaladina, where the already-cooked onions are baked on bread dough and garnished with black olives. The recipe I am giving here is from Lorraine.

Make a short crust with generous 1¾ cups of flour, ½ cup of butter, a pinch of salt, and a little water. Let it rest while preparing 1½–2 pounds of sliced onions; melt them gently in butter. This will take about 30 minutes, with the pan covered. Take them off the fire, and stir in 2 beaten eggs, and ½ cup of grated Gruyère cheese. Roll out the dough, spread it on a tart pan (9–10 inches), fill up with the onion mixture, and bake it in a moderate oven (350°F) for 20 to 30 minutes.

Enough for six.

A pizza in the Roman way

In the pizzeria where I used often to eat when I spent a winter in Rome 25 years ago, by far the best pizza was spread only with onions stewed in olive oil and seasoned with oregano. The Romans themselves claim this as the only true pizza, and dismiss the tomato and mozzarella version of Naples as a fanciful upstart.

For a 8½–9½-inch pizza, the ingredients for the dough are generous 1 cup of plain unbleached bread flour, 1 teaspoon of salt, ¼ ounce of fresh yeast, 2–3 tablespoons of olive oil, 4–5 tablespoons of milk, 1 whole egg. For the filling you need about 1½ pounds of onion cut into fine rings, olive oil, salt, and oregano.

Warm the flour and salt. Mix the yeast to a cream with 2 tablespoons of the tepid milk. Break the egg into the center of the flour. Pour in the creamed yeast and 2 tablespoons of olive oil. Mix to a light soft dough. If too dry, add the rest of the milk and another tablespoon of oil. Form into a ball. Cover with a sheet of plastic wrap and leave in a warm place to rise. Allow 2 hours.

Stew the onions slowly, slowly, in fruity olive oil until quite soft and yellow. Season with salt and a good sprinkling of oregano.

When the dough is ready, that is when it has just about trebled in volume and is light and puffy, break it down, shape it into a ball, and pat it out into a 8½-inch disk on a perfectly flat, oiled fireproof platter, or on a baking sheet.

Spread the warm onions on the dough, leaving a little uncovered around the outer edge. Scatter a little more oregano and a little more olive oil over the filling and let rise for 15 to 20 minutes before putting it into the center of the oven to bake. Temperature should be fairly hot, 425°F, and the pizza will take from 20 to 25 minutes to cook.

There will be enough for two to four, depending on appetite and what else you have for the meal.

BREADS

A coburg or round loaf

¼ ounce of fresh yeast or 1 teaspoon active dry yeast, rather under ½ ounce salt, and slightly under generous 1 cup of warm water, 3 cups of white bread flour. Also needed is a floured baking sheet or heatproof earthenware platter.

Mix the fresh yeast to a cream with a little tepid water. Stir the active dry yeast and salt into the flour, put the bowl, covered, into a very low oven for 5 minutes, just long enough to warm the flour. Mix the creamed yeast into it, add the tepid water. The right temperature is about 98.6° to 100.4°F. Mix well and shape the dough into a ball. If it is too wet, sprinkle with a little more flour. Cover, and leave in a warm place to rise. The ideal temperature is from 69.8° to 73.4°F.

In an hour to an hour and a half the dough should have doubled in volume and feel spongy and light. Scoop it up, and slap it down hard in the bowl or on a board. Repeat this three or four times. The more the dough is knocked down at this stage, the better the loaf will be.

Now knead and roll the dough into a ball, place this in the center of the floured baking sheet. At this stage—and it is an important one—fold the ball of dough all around, tucking the edges underneath so that the uncooked loaf looks like a little round, plump pillow. If this detail is omitted, the loaf will spread out flat. Getting the shape right is a knack which may take a few tries to acquire. The correct consistency of the dough also plays an important part. If it is too wet nothing will prevent it from spreading, so if you have used too much water sprinkle in more flour as you shape the loaf. Try not to overdo the addition of flour, or the finished loaf will turn out patchy.

It is advisable to cover the dough while it is rising for the second time and the easiest way to do this is to invert a clean bowl over it. For example, quickly rinse and dry the bowl used for mixing the dough. Don't use it without cleaning it; an hour later it will be twice as difficult to wash. An alternative method is to put the shaped ball of dough upside down into the floured bowl, and cover it with a plate or a floured cloth.

Three-quarters of an hour should be long enough for the dough to double its volume once again. Remove the covering bowl. If necessary reshape the loaf. (If you have used the method of rising the loaf upside down in a bowl, simply invert it onto the baking sheet.) With a sharp knife or scissors make three deepish cuts, one right across the loaf, the other two from the outer edges inward to the center, so that they meet the first cut and form a cross. As the cuts open, the loaf is ready to go into the oven.

Have the oven heated to 450°F. Bake the loaf on the center shelf for 15 minutes at this temperature, another 15 at 400°F, then turn it upside down and leave for 10 to 15 minutes with the oven turned off.

Cool on a rack.

NOTES AND VARIATIONS:

1. If this loaf is baked plain, without cuts, it is called a cob, an old word meaning "head." Basically, it is just the ordinary round loaf baked on the brick oven floor since the earliest times. A variation in cuts is a checkerboard pattern, called a "rumpy."

2. Any number of permutations on flour mixtures can be used for this loaf. I have given the recipe using all white bread flour because that is the easiest flour for a beginner to work with. A mixture of white bread flour and whole wheat also makes good coburgs and cobs.

3. Lightweight nonstick oven sheets are useful for baking hand-shaped loaves. These sheets are rather small, so it is a good idea to have two which fit side by side on the oven shelf.

4. An experienced bread maker will know that generous 2¾ cups of strong plain bread flour can be leavened with ¼ ounce of yeast only. If you need to hurry the dough, then use ½ ounce of yeast, but the slower rising with less yeast will make a better loaf. Alternatively, you can make two loaves, or one large one, with scant 5¾ cups of flour but still using only the ½ ounce of yeast.

Salted and spiced bread strips or ribbons

To make about three dozen strips, quantities are generous 3½ cups of white flour (ordinary plain can be used), ½ ounce of fresh yeast or 2 teaspoons active dry yeast, scant 2 cups of milk, 2 tablespoons of butter, 2 teaspoons of salt. For adding to the dough after the rising: 2 teaspoons of fennel seeds, cumin seeds, or caraway seeds, whichever you prefer. For strewing over the ribbons before baking: extra salt, preferably in coarse crystal form, and a few more seeds, and for brushing the dough, a little milk.

Put the flour, salt, and active dry yeast if you are using it, into a bowl. Cream the fresh yeast with a little of the warm milk, stir it into the flour, then add the rest of the warm milk and butter. Mix to a fairly firm, smooth, and flexible dough. Cover and let rise for about an hour, or until at least doubled in volume, and very puffy and light. Knock the dough down, knead it a little, working in the warmed seeds as you do so. Divide it into two equal portions. Press each of these out flat on a floured board or baking sheet (if you have a nonstick one, it is just the thing for this type of dough), then with a rolling pin, roll the dough into a rectangle, as neatly and evenly shaped as you can manage.

Repeat the process with the second portion of dough. If your rectangles of dough have been rolled out on a board, transfer them to a floured baking sheet. With a sharp knife, make one cut right through the center of each rectangle, from one side to the other. Then working from top to bottom, cut long strips, about 1 inch in width, so that the whole rectangle is literally cut to ribbons, but left in its original shape.

Brush the ribbons with milk, scatter a few more seeds over them, and add a good sprinkling of coarse salt. Leave the dough to recover its spring. This will take about 15 to 30 minutes.

Have the oven heated to 400°F and bake the ribbons on the center shelf for 15 minutes, and for another 5 minutes on the lowest shelf.

By the time the ribbons are cooked, they will have puffed up, expanded, and almost rejoined themselves into one rectangle of bread; they are, however, easily broken apart, and can be piled lightly onto a dish or in a basket. They are delicious while still warm, with soft mild cheeses and with rough red wine.

Cheese and dill sticks

A richer, puffier dough than the one used for salted and spiced ribbons, and a really excellent confection to offer with white wine.

For the first trial, make a small quantity as follows: generous 1¾ cups white bread flour, 2 teaspoons of salt, ¼ ounce of fresh yeast or 1 teaspoon of active dry yeast, ½ cup of butter, 6 tablespoons of cream, 3 teaspoons of dill seeds, 2–3 ounces of a soft melting cheese such as Bel Paese, Port Salut, or Gruyère, a little extra cream for brushing the dough.

Put the flour, salt, and active dry yeast in a bowl, cream the fresh yeast with a little water. Warm the butter until it is quite soft. Rub it into the flour. Add the creamed yeast, then mix to a light dough with the warmed cream. Form it into a ball, cover, and let rise until it is light and puffy, and at least doubled in volume.

Strew a little flour on a nonstick baking sheet. Break down the dough, rather gently, scatter in two teaspoons of the dill seeds. Put the dough on the floured baking sheet, press it out into a rectangle roughly 9 x 7 inches, then with a rolling pin, roll it out quite evenly. On it strew the cheese, cut into tiny cubes. Fold the dough into three. Roll out and fold again, twice, rather as if for puff pastry or croissant dough, but very quickly and lightly, and without waiting to rest between each turn.

Finally, when you have rolled the dough out into a 9 x 7-inch rectangle for the fourth time, make three lengthwise cuts right through the dough, then 10 to 12 cuts the other way. The cuts should go right through the dough.

Brush the surface with a little cream or milk, sprinkle the remaining teaspoon of dill seeds on the top, cover with a light cloth, and let the dough recover, about 30 minutes.

Bake in the center of the oven, 400°F, for 15 minutes, and for another 10 minutes on the bottom shelf at the same temperature. (If you intend reheating the sticks, take them out after the first 15 minutes, and reheat them on the bottom shelf when convenient.)

During the baking, the sticks join themselves together again but are still clearly defined so that is is a matter of seconds to divide them, making neat portions.

DESSERTS

Lemon ice cream

2 lemons, ¾ cup confectioners' sugar, ⅔ cup heavy cream.

Put the thinly peeled rind of the lemons with the confectioners' sugar in 1½ cups of water, and simmer gently for 20 minutes. Let the syrup cool, strain, and add to it the juice of the lemons. When quite cold, add it gradually to the whipped cream, stirring gently until the whole mixture is smooth.

Pour into the ice tray or use an ice-cream maker. If using ice trays, cover with foil and freeze for 2½ to 3 hours, taking it out to stir twice, after the first half hour, and again after another hour.

Enough for three to four.

Orange ice cream

Natillas, the Spanish custard, is made with far fewer eggs to milk than the usual French, Italian, and English equivalents. It makes a light and delicate ice cream and, the proportions and method once mastered, there is really no limit to the variations of flavoring which may be made.

First the custard: ingredients for 4 cups of mixture are 3 cups of milk, a strip of orange peel, a piece of cinnamon bark or a teaspoon of ground cinnamon, scant ⅓ cup of sugar, 2 whole eggs and 2 yolks. Additional ingredients are generous ¾ cup of cream, grated orange or tangerine peel, and perhaps more cinnamon.

Put the milk, strip of orange peel, cinnamon, and sugar in a heavy saucepan of 1.5 quart capacity. Bring to simmering point.

Have the eggs ready and well beaten in a bowl, or whirled in the blender. Over them strain the hot milk mixture and beat or whirl the mixture again. Return it to the rinsed pan.

Cook the *natillas* over very gentle heat, whisking continuously until the custard starts to thicken. Remove the saucepan from the heat and either continue whisking until the custard is cool or give it another whirl in the blender. Chill in the refrigerator.

Now the ice cream: immediately before freezing, whirl the custard once more in the blender, adding the generous ¾ cup of cream and a little extra cinnamon and finely grated orange or tangerine peel.

Enough for six to eight.

Mango sorbet

To make 4 cups of this delicious ice you need 4 or 5 fine ripe mangoes, a thin syrup made with scant ⅓ cup of sugar to ⅔ cup of water, ⅔ cup of cream, about 2 tablespoons of lemon juice.

Peel the mangoes and slice all the flesh into a bowl, scraping as much as possible from the seeds. Puree it in the blender. There should be 22–24 ounces of fruit pulp. Add the cold sugar syrup and the lemon juice. Immediately before freezing blend in the cream.

Enough for six to eight.

Strawberry granita

Now that we can buy strawberries nearly all the year around, a strawberry sorbet would seem to be the best basic one to know. Mine is the Italian version. It contains orange juice, which brings out the flavor of the strawberries in a remarkable way, giving the mixture an intensity and concentration of scent not otherwise to be achieved with any but the finest fresh strawberries.

Quantities are 2 pounds of strawberries, the juice of half a lemon and of half an orange, 1¼ cups white sugar, ⅔ cup of water.

Hull the strawberries, puree them in the blender, press them through a stainless-steel or nylon strainer (wire discolors the fruit). Add the strained orange and lemon juice.

Boil the sugar and water for about 7 minutes to make a thin syrup (to make a sorbet of greater density, boil the syrup for 10 minutes, or until it is beginning to thicken) and let it cool before adding it to the strawberry pulp.

Chill the mixture before turning it into the refrigerator trays to freeze, which will take 2 to 2½ hours at the normal ice-making temperature. Keep the trays tightly covered with foil during the freezing process, and transfer them from the ice compartment to the less cold part of the refrigerator for about 10 minutes before dividing up the ice and serving it.

As the name implies, this type of water ice should be slightly grainy, no more than just barely frozen. The quantities given should be enough for six to eight helpings. Serve with French boudoir cookies or ladyfingers.

Tarte aux pommes normande
Open apple tart

Peel and core 1½ pounds sweet apples and slice them rather thinly and evenly. Melt 3 tablespoons butter in a skillet, put in your apples, add 3 or 4 tablespoons of white sugar (vanilla-flavored if you like), and cook gently until the apples are pale golden and transparent. Turn the slices over gently so as not to break them, and, if they are very closely packed, shake the pan rather than stir the apples.

Make a *pâté sablée* or crumbly pie dough by rubbing 6 tablespoons of butter into 1¼ cups of all-purpose flour, a quarter-teaspoon of salt, and 3 teaspoons of white sugar. Moisten with 2 to 4 tablespoons of ice-cold water. If it is still too dry, add a little more, but the less water you use, the more crumbly and light your pie dough will be.

Simply shape the dough into a ball and immediately, without letting it rest or rolling it out, spread it with your hands into a lightly buttered 8-inch flat pan. Brush the edges with thin cream or milk; arrange the apples, without the juice, in overlapping circles, keeping a nicely shaped piece for the center. Bake, with the pan on a baking sheet in a preheated hot oven at 400°F, for 30 to 35 minutes, turning the pan around once during the cooking. Take it from the oven, pour in the buttery juices, which have been reheated, give another sprinkling of sugar, and return to the oven for barely a minute.

Although it is at its best hot, this pastry will not go sodden even when it is cold.

Enough for four to six.

Gâteau au chocolat et aux amandes
Chocolate and almond cake

¼ pound of bitter chocolate, 1 teaspoon each of rum or brandy and black coffee, 6 tablespoons of butter, ¼ cup of superfine sugar, 1 cup of ground almonds, 3 eggs.

Break the chocolate into small pieces; put them with the rum and coffee to melt in a cool oven. Stir the mixture well. Put it with the butter, sugar, and ground almonds in a saucepan and stir over low fire for a few minutes until all of the ingredients are blended smoothly together. Off the heat, stir in the well-beaten egg yolks, and then fold in the stiffly whipped whites. Turn into a lightly buttered shallow sponge-cake pan, of 7–8 inches diameter, or a tart pan with a removable bottom, stand the pan on a baking sheet, and cook in a very low oven, 275°F, for about 45 minutes. This cake, owing to the total absence of flour, is rather fragile, so turn it out, when it is cool, with the utmost caution. It can either be served as it is, or covered with lightly whipped and sweetened cream. It is a cake which is equally good for dessert or for teatime.

Enough for six.

Budino di ricotta
Ricotta dessert

This is really more like a light, soft cake than a dessert. In fact it is the very nicest and most delicate cheesecake filling without the pie dough.

Ingredients are: generous 1¾ cups of ricotta, 1 heaping tablespoon of flour, 4 whole eggs, 4 tablespoons of sugar, a pinch of salt, 1 tablespoon of candied orange or lemon peel, the grated zest of a small lemon, 2 teaspoons of powdered cinnamon, 3 tablespoons of rum.

Press the ricotta through a fine stainless-steel wire or nylon strainer. (This operation will only take a minute or two.) Stir in the flour, 1 whole egg, 3 tablespoons of sugar, the salt, candied peel, lemon zest, and 1 teaspoon of cinnamon. Separate the remaining three eggs. Beat the yolks with the rum. Incorporate the ricotta mixture. Have ready a plain cake pan of 6⅓ cups capacity), preferably a nonstick one, buttered and floured. Set the oven to moderate, 350°F.

Now whisk the egg whites until they stand in soft peaks. Quickly fold them into the main mixture and pour it into the pan. Give the pan a light tap against the table to eliminate air pockets. Bake the cake for 45 to 50 minutes, just below the center of the oven. The batter rises quite a bit (hence the seemingly overlarge pan) but should turn only a very pale gold, not brown. Cream-cheese batters burn easily, so take a look after the first 25 minutes of cooking, and if necessary reduce the oven heat. When the cake is just beginning to come away from the sides of the pan, it is done. Let it cool before turning it out onto a plate or flat dish. Eat cold. Just before serving, sprinkle the top with the reserved sugar and cinnamon, mixed together.

Enough for four to six.

Spiced prunes

To make this excellent and useful dessert it is essential to use whole spices. Ground ones won't do at all.

For 1 pound of large prunes the spices needed are: two 2-inch pieces of cinnamon or cassia bark, 2 level teaspoons of coriander seeds, 2 blades of mace, 4 whole cloves.

Put the prunes and spices in a bowl or earthenware casserole. Just cover them with cold water. Leave overnight. Next day cook the prunes in an uncovered casserole in a low oven or over very moderate direct heat until they are swollen but not mushy. About half the cooking water will have evaporated. Take out the fruit and remove the pits.

Heat up the remaining juice with the spices, until it is slightly syrupy. Pour it through a strainer over the prunes.

To be eaten cold, with cream or yogurt, or with the cabbage dish on page 159.

NOTES

1. Cassia is a variant of cinnamon. The two are very easily distinguishable. Cinnamon quills are long, smooth, and curled, cassia bark is rough and comes in large chips. Although often held to be inferior to cinnamon, there are those—among them some Pakistani cooks—who consider cassia the better of the two. Confusion arises, however, because Pakistani spice sellers and cooks insist that cassia bark is cinnamon.

2. Mace is the beautiful orange lacy covering of the nutmeg. When dried it turns pale tawny in color and is very hard. It is marketed in broken pieces called blades. These give out a wonderful aroma in cooking. Unfortunately, most people buy mace in powder form and so have no notion whatever of its true character. In this dish of spiced prunes there is no substitute for whole mace.

3. An alternative way of using spiced prunes is to leave them in the turned-off oven after they are cooked. By the time the oven is cold, the prunes have soaked up nearly all the juice. They are fat and swollen. Serve them as they are, without pitting them, as an after-dinner sweetmeat.

INDEX

Publishing director: Jane O'Shea
Creative director: Helen Lewis
Editor: Jill Norman
Project editor: Simon Davis
Art direction and design: Lawrence Morton
Photographer: Kristin Perers
Props stylist: Cynthia Inions
Production director: Vincent Smith
Production controller: Sasha Taylor

VIKING STUDIO
Published by the Penguin Group
Penguin Group (USA) Inc., 375 Hudson Street,
New York, New York 10014, USA

USA / Canada / UK / Ireland / Australia /
New Zealand / India / South Africa / China

Penguin Books Ltd, Registered Offices: 80 Strand,
London WC2R 0RL, England
For more information about the Penguin Group
visit penguin.com

First published in Great Britain by Quadrille
Publishing Limited

"Brown Oatmeal Bread," "A Coburg or Round
Loaf," "Irish Wholemeal Soda Bread," and "White
Buttermilk Bread" from *English Bread and
Yeast Cookery* by Elizabeth David. Copyright ©
Elizabeth David, 1977. Used by permission of
Viking Penguin, a member of Penguin Group
(USA) Inc.
"Aubergines with Garlic," "Budino di Ricotta,"
"Cheese and Dill Sticks," "Garlic Presses Are
Utterly Useless," "Giulia's Tomato Sauce and Dry
Rice," "Gratin of Rice and Courgettes," "The Great
English Aphrodisiac," "Green Vegetable Risotto,"
"Leaf Salads," "Mango Sorbet," "Orange Ice
Cream," "Pasternak and Cress Cream," "A Pizza in
the Roman Way," "Salsa Marinara," "Salted Bread
Sticks," "Strawberry Granita," "Tomatoes with
Rice and Walnut Stuffing," "Tuscan Bean Soup,"
and "Vegetable Risotto" from *Is There a Nutmeg
in the House?* by Elizabeth David. Copyright ©
The Estate of Elizabeth David, 2000. Used by
permission of Viking Penguin, a member of
Penguin Group (USA) Inc.

"Waiting for Lunch," "Trufflesville Regis," and
"Bruscandoli" appeared in Elizabeth David's *An
Omelette and a Glass of Wine.*

ISBN 978-0-670-01668-6

Printed in China
10 9 8 7 6 5 4 3 2 1